To Dream Again

"Where there is no vision, the people perish"
Proverbs 29: 18

Central Baptist Church   George Evans 2010

Helen M. Martin

AuthorHouse™
1663 Liberty Drive
Bloomington, IN 47403
www.authorhouse.com
Phone: 833-262-8899

Because of the dynamic nature of the Internet, any web addresses or links contained in this book may have changed since publication and may no longer be valid. The views expressed in this work are solely those of the author and do not necessarily reflect the views of the publisher, and the publisher hereby disclaims any responsibility for them.

Any people depicted in stock imagery provided by Getty Images are models, and such images are being used for illustrative purposes only.
Certain stock imagery © Getty Images.

This book is printed on acid-free paper.

ISBN: 979-8-8230-1803-6 (sc)
ISBN: 979-8-8230-1805-0 (hc)
ISBN: 979-8-8230-1804-3 (e)

Library of Congress Control Number: 2023922541

Print information available on the last page.

Published by AuthorHouse 10/21/2024

authorHOUSE®

To Dream Again

"Where there is no vision, the people perish"
Proverbs 29: 18

HELEN M. MARTIN
The Author

Central Baptist Church   *George Evans 2010*

Helen M. Martin

TO DREAM AGAIN

"Where there is no vision, the
people perish"
Proverbs 29: 18

The book is divided into parts. The
first part is the church history. The
second is the story of the beautiful
stained glass windows and the
people who were honored with one
dedicated to them.

The purpose of this history is to
update events for almost 135 years
of Central Baptist Church and it's
service to the people of Gainesville,
Georgia and the Hall County area.
It covers in decade format what has
taken place as it began as a house
of worship, and events as it

Helen lives in Gainesville, Georgia. She is
a graduate of Brenau University in
Gainesville, and the University of Georgia
in Athens, Georgia. She is retired from the
Gainesville City Schools where she taught
and worked as an administrator. Since her
retirement her passion remains working
with children and interviewing veterans for
the Library of Congress. She is also a
member of the Northeast Georgia History
Center, and serves as Church Historian,
Director of Sunday School and Vacation
Bible School for many years. She is an
avid member of of Colonel William Candler
Chapter, NSDAR, Joseph Royall Chapter,
Colonel Dames of The XVII Century, the
Jamestown Society and the Magna Charta
Society. Helen has published a novel, a
historical book on North Green Street,
published poems, and illustrated a poetry
book.

George Evans is an artist.
The rendering on the front cover
of the book and the dust jacket
was a gift to our church in 2010.
He works in Architectural
Illustration and Design.

George Evans

PASTOR MIKE TAYLOR

Words are so inefficient
to show how much
friends like the three of
you mean to me with a
task of this magnitude.
The typing assistance
and the editing was a
daunting task. I guess
thank you very much
from Helen and all of
Central must suffice.

DOT FLOYD   **GRACE KEMP**

Dedicated to the memory of Truman Collier Skaggs and Dorothy Dean Skaggs, pastor and wife of Central Baptist Church from 1978 to 1993. Pastor Truman was a prayer warrior and outstanding leader. Dorothy Skaggs taught Sunday School, and participated in all church activities.

TRUMAN COLLIER SKAGGS   DOROTHY DEAN PORTER SKAGGS

March 4, 1928-April 14, 2017   March 11, 1925 - January 9, 2016

The baptismal widow was purchased in 1930 by the WMU for $275.

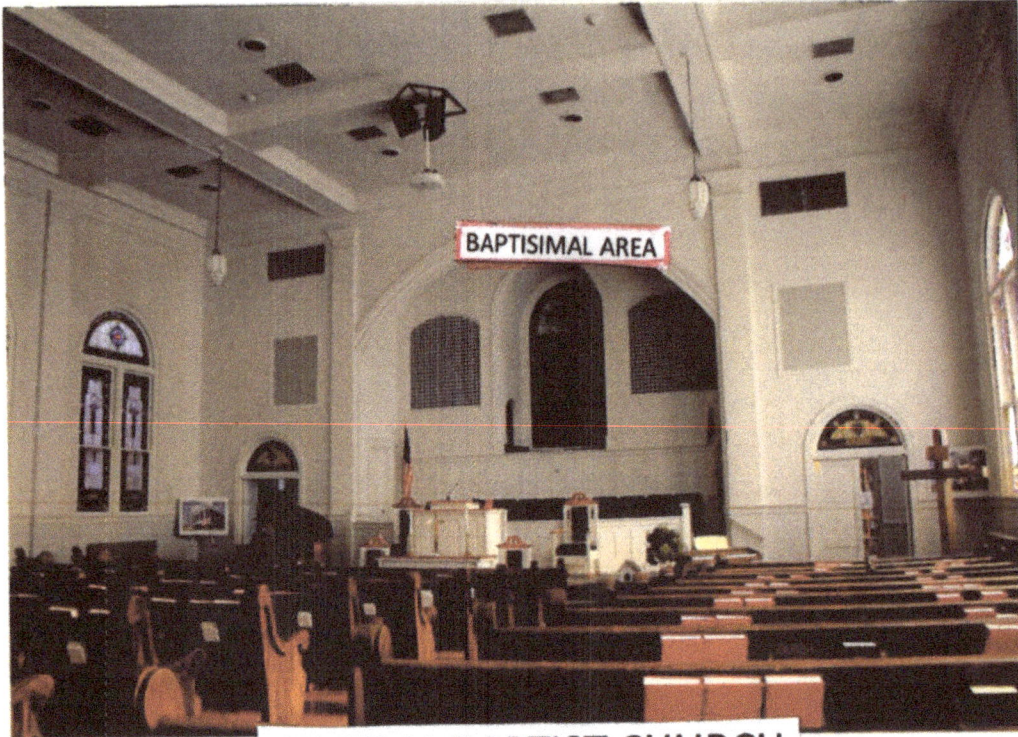

BAPTISIMAL AREA

CENTRAL BAPTIST CHURCH

There are ten sets of these windows in the church sanctuary.

There are four of these single windows in the church.

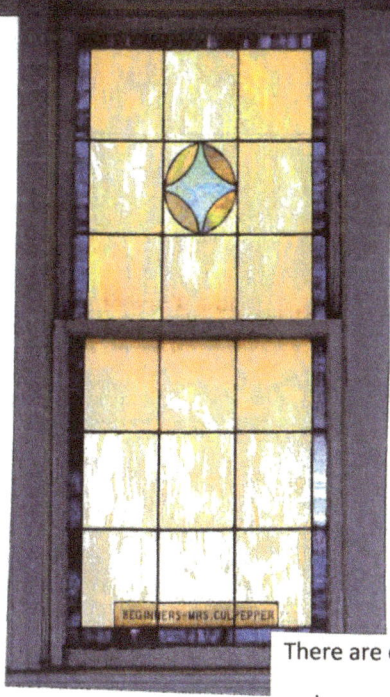

There are dozens of these windows and many other sizes over doors and exits.

Central Baptist Church
785 Main Street
Gainesville, Georgia

(ADMINISTRATIVE OFFICES AND MEDIA CENTER)   (FELLOWSHIP HALL AND EDUCATIONAL BUILDING)

8/21/2018

BACK ENTRY TO THE CHURCH AND THE ELEVATOR

To Dream Again

"Where there is no vision, the people perish"
Proverbs 29: 18

Helen M. Martin

TABLE OF CONTENTS

PREFACE

The purpose of this brief history of Central Baptist Church is to update church events since the publication of Dr. Harold F. Green's book **NOT MADE FOR DEFEAT.** Also, it is an attempt to summarize in concise form church historical events during Central's first century and beyond.

I have chosen the title **TO DREAM AGAIN** because it presents a note of optimism and reminds us as a great Christian people we can learn from the past, but we cannot live in it. The subtitle of this history is taken from Proverbs 29: 18.

God used visions and dreams to reveal His plans, to further His plans, and to put people in places of influence. This was clear as people came forward in times of money distress, and building decisions to be made. The building of Central was undertaken by God's people following His plan.

I believe three quotes from persons dedicated to Central's well-being captures the spirit of optimism.

From the words of Dr. Harold F. Green...

"It is true that one day Central could die, but her indominable spirit never will. In fact, many feel that she will never die because she was not made for defeat." 1974

From Truman C. Skaggs, the longest tenured pastor... 1993

"Go ye into all the world and preach the gospel to every creature.

Central Baptist Church has celebrated more than a century as a Baptist Church dedicated to this clarion mission."

From Mike Taylor, Pastor, "On the last Sunday in January 2020, we celebrated 130 years of service to the Lord, and we continue to reach out to our community, our county, and beyond."

"Where there is no vision, the people perish." Proverbs 29: 18.

Love, Helen

INTRODUCTION

Central Baptist Church is a caring, dedicated people who must work toward the task of reaching an inner city and community for Christ. We must be committed to dream again—to come alive! As the Bible teaches us, dreams have an impact when set in motion. We must lead people into becoming a dynamic force for the kingdom's work. We must look to God to make this a reality.

Part I of this book about Central gives an overview of events by decades with many note-worthy events of the one-hundred thirty plus years of of its history.

Part II of the book has information on the people who have been blessed to have a window dedicated to them. Miss Alline Johnson served as treasurer of the first Window Building Fund. Many community canvas projects were conducted with appeals for assistance during the building years from 1925 until 1932. She was a dedicated servant of the Lord and loved Central. She died in 1969, and Dr. Harold F. Green conducted her memorial service.

The second appeal for marking some unmarked windows was supervised by Jan Alton Cobb. There were areas in the aging church that needed some updating. The money that was given to add names on existing windows was used to have new pew cushions in the sanctuary, and other repairs.

It became this church historian's dream to put as much information about the church history and facts about the people as could be found in the minute books of the church. Our church was dedicated as a National Treasure and Historical Site by the Colonial Dames of the Seventeenth Century on September 9, 2020.

CHESTNUT STREET-- THE MISSION

Chestnut Street Mission work began in March 1890 in the schoolhouse of Miss Amanda McCants. The mission was started by Rev. J. L. R. Barrett, W. M. Hadaway, W. A. Brown, S. C. Kicklighter, W. S. Battle, J. C. Otwell and others whose names were remembered by J. C Otwell, church clerk, on January 31, 1891.

The mission was assisted by the First Baptist Church. From March 1890, to January 30, 1891, services were held every Sunday Afternoon with Sunday School and preaching. There was a prayer meeting every Tuesday night. There was a series of meetings, dates not recorded, which lasted for thirteen days. During these there were often so many people the schoolhouse would not hold them. These meetings were aided by the pastor of the First Baptist Church, Rev. F. C. McConnell, and Revs. M. D. Hudson and Thomas O'Kelly.

CHESTNUT STREET MISSION
March 1890

CHESTNUT STREET BAPTIST
CHURCH
January 30, 1891

From the pen of J. C. Otwell, first church clerk. . . page 1. . .

"Upon the 30th day of January, 1891, a Presbytery, consisting of Revs. A. Van Hoose, F. E. McConnell and J. L. R. Barrett was convened at this mission school house and the mission terminated in what was then known as "Chestnut Street Baptist Church." With Rev. J. L. R. Barrett as pastor for the year 1891. And thus we bid adieu to our loved "Chestnut Street Mission" and enter the field as a Church, with Christ our living Head.

Grimesville, Ga., Jan. 31, 1891.

J. C. Otwell
Ch. Clerk

CHESTNUT STREET BAPTIST CHURCH

The first service of Chestnut Street Baptist Church was held on January 30, 1891, after the church had been constituted. Rev. J. L. Phillips delivered the sermon. A conference followed the sermon with Rev. J. L. R. Barrett, moderator, and J. C. Otwell, clerk. After the "Articles of Faith," "Church Order" and "Church Covenant" were read and accepted, the church was declared a regularly constituted church.

Business: Notes below copied directly from J. C. Otwell, First Clerk's, minutes on January 30, 1891.

1. The door of the church was opened and no one joined.
2. Rev. J. L. R. Barrett was unanimously chosen as pastor for 1891.
3. Bro. J. C. Otwell was unanimously elected church clerk for 1891.
4. A Building Committee was appointed by the moderator. Those appointed were Brethren W. M. Hadaway, J. C. Otwell, W. M. Coker, S.R. Tally and W. P. Pirkle. The moderator was added by a motion.
5. The clerk was instructed to purchase a suitable record book for the church.
6. Brethren Hadaway and Coker responded to a call by the moderator to serve as sextons, church officers responsible for the care and upkeep of church property.
7. The "Rules of Decorum "and "Order of Business" were read and unanimously adopted.
8. The first Sunday in each month was set as the regular "Meeting Day."
9. Regular conference to be held on the first Tuesday night of each month.

----In June 1892, the church moved into the first Church building. On June 1, 1903, the church building was completely destroyed by a tornado.

TITLE DEED.

THE STATE OF GEORGIA, *Hall* COUNTY.

THIS INDENTURE, Made this 16th day of April in the year of our Lord One Thousand Eight Hundred and *Ninety one* between *G. A. Dozier* of the County of *Hall* and State of Georgia of the *first* part, and *J. L. R. Barrett, J. C. Otwell, M. M. Anderson, Wm ___ ___* *Trustees and other members of Chestnut Street Baptist ___* of the County of *Hall* and State of *Georgia* of the other part, WITNESSETH: That the said *party of the first part* for and in consideration of the sum of *Fifty* DOLLARS

in hand paid, at and before the sealing and delivery of these presents, the receipt whereof is hereby acknowledged, ha__ granted, bargained, sold and conveyed, and by these presents do__ grant, bargain, sell and convey unto the said *parties of the second part their* heirs and assigns, all that *tract or parcel of land situated, lying and being in* the *following described property, to-wit: All that tract or parcel of land situate, lying and being in the City of Gainesville said County and State and fronting on the East side Chestnut street and Commencing at the corner of Mrs. Emily Means lot on said street, thence in a Southerly direction along said street fifty feet; thence running back from said street in an Easterly direction one hundred feet; thence in a Northerly direction fifty feet to said Mrs. Means line; thence along Mrs. Means line in a Westerly direction one hundred feet to the beginning corner And bounded on North by Mrs. Emily Means on the West by said Chestnut Street and upon the South and East by the lands of R. Smith & G. A. Dozier.*

to granted and described property with all and singular the rights, members and appurtenances thereof, to the same being and belonging, or in anywise appertaining, to the only proper use, benefit and behoof of the said *party of the second part their* heirs, executors, administrators and assigns, in fee-simple; and the said *party of the first part the said bargained property above described* heirs, executors, and administrators, unto the said *party of the second part their* heirs, executors, administrators and assigns, against the said *party of the first part their* heirs, executors, and administrators, and all and every other person or persons shall and will warrant and forever defend, by virtue of these presents.

IN WITNESS WHEREOF, The said *party of the second part* __ __ hereto set their hand__ and affixed their seal__ the day and year first above written.

Signed, sealed and delivered in presence of

H. H. ___   5   *R. Smith* (SEAL)

H. ___   *G. A. Dozier* (SEAL)

      (SEAL)

Recorded this 21 day of April 189 *H. R. Smith* CLERK.

TORNADO-----JUNE 1, 1903

Around 200 were killed 90 years ago

GAINESVILLE, Ga. — A most terrific cyclone, about 100 yards in width, passed over the southern portion of the city at 1 o'clock Monday afternoon, leaving death and destruction in its path.

Houses and trees were swept from the face of the earth as if they were chaff.

The cyclone made terrific noise, as if heavy cannonading were in full blast, and as it bore down upon the city, it tore everything in its path.

— The Gainesville News,
June 3, 1903.

By A.J. Banks
The Times

Storm still draws fear years later

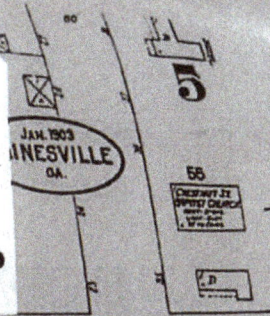

HIGH STREET

JAN. 1903
GAINESVILLE
GA.

— #2
First
Church

← High Street
January 1903
June1, 1903 – Destroyed
by tornado

BRADFORD

CHESTNUT

From June, 1903, until 1904, worship services were held in Hobbs Chapel, a house located on Summit Street.

Tracking the "Cyclone of '03"

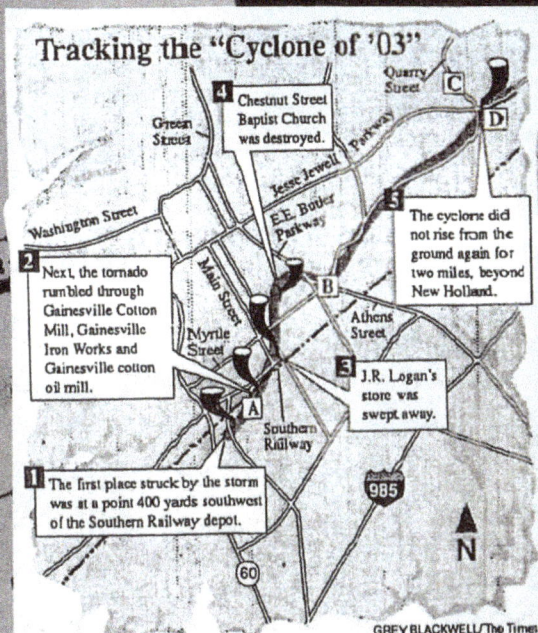

Quarry Street

4 Chestnut Street Baptist Church was destroyed.

Green Street

Jesse Jewell Parkway

E.E. Butler Parkway

5 The cyclone did not rise from the ground again for two miles, beyond New Holland.

Washington Street

Main Street

Myrtle Street

Athens Street

2 Next, the tornado rumbled through Gainesville Cotton Mill, Gainesville Iron Works and Gainesville cotton oil mill.

3 J.R. Logan's store was swept away.

Southern Railway

1 The first place struck by the storm was at a point 400 yards southwest of the Southern Railway depot.

985

60

N

GREY BLACKWELL/The Times

6

THE SECOND CHURCH BUILDING-----MYRTLE AND MAPLE STREETS

The congregation moved into its new church building in 1904. The church had used a home, Hobbs' Chapel, located on Summit Street during the time the new church was being constructed. The church was wired for electricity in 1905, one of the first to be wired.

On April 6, 1904, the church unanimously voted to change its name to

CENTRAL BAPTIST CHURCH.

Central Baptist Church
Myrtle and Maple Streets
1904 - December 5, 1926

116

State of Georgia, Hall County.

In consideration of the sum of Five Hundred Dollars, to me paid, I, Z. T. Castleberry of the County of Hall and State of Georgia, do hereby sell and convey unto John T. Waters B. F. Roberts and L. A. Jones, Trustees of Chestnut Street Baptist Church, and their successors in office, of the County of Hall and State of Georgia their heirs and assigns, a tract or parcel of land which is described as follows:- Beginning at a stake on the corner of Maple and Myrtle Streets in the City of Gainesville, Georgia, and running south along the West side of Myrtle Street, One hundred and thirty five (135) feet to a twenty (20) foot Alley, thence along said Alley North West One hundred and twenty eight (128) feet to a stake, thence North East One hundred and thirty five (135) feet, parallel to Myrtle Street, to a stake on Maple Street; thence South East along said Maple Street One hundred and twenty eight (128) feet to the beginning corner. Said lots being lots Nos. 5 and 6 of the Sub-division of the Z. T. Castleberry property-

To have and to hold said land and appurtenances unto said John T. Waters, B. T. Roberts and L. A. Jones Trustees of Chestnut Street Baptist Church and their successors in office, heirs, executors, administrators and assigns, in fee simple.

I warrant the title to said land against the lawful claims of ~~each~~ all persons-

In Witness Whereof, I have hereunto set my hand & affixed my seal, this the 8th day of October 1903-

Signed, sealed & delivered
in presence of
J. T. Telford.
B. H. Whelchel, Notary Public
  Hall County, Georgia.

Z. T. Castleberry - (Seal)

Recorded, Oct. 8th 1903.
  Jno M. Bell, C.S.C.

State of Georgia, Hall County.

In consideration of the sum of One Hundred & Twenty five Dollars, to me paid, I, L. H. Naywood of the County of Hall and State of Georgia do hereby sell and convey unto M. B. H. Telford of the County of Hall and State of Georgia, her heirs & assigns, a tract or parcel of land which is described as follows:- All that tract or parcel of land known as lot No. 3, Felix Brown plat, lying in the City of Gainesville, County of Hall and State of Georgia,

GRANTOR
Z. T. CASTLEBERRY

October 8, 1903

GRANTEES
JOHN T WATERS
B. F. ROBERTS
L. A. JONES
TRUSTEES

8

2nd Church
corner of Maple and
Myrtle Street
(Lots 5,6)

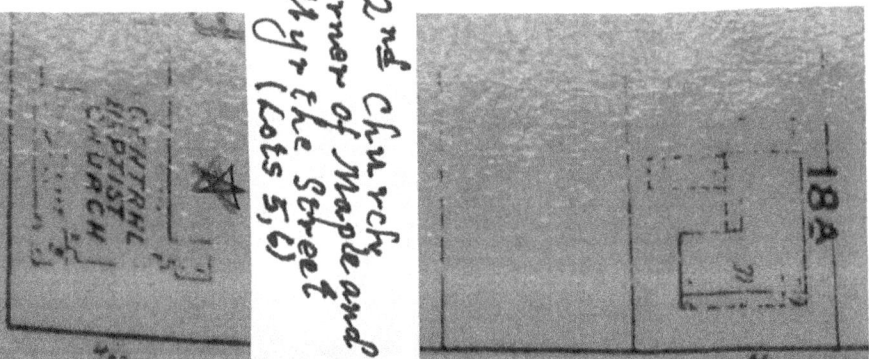

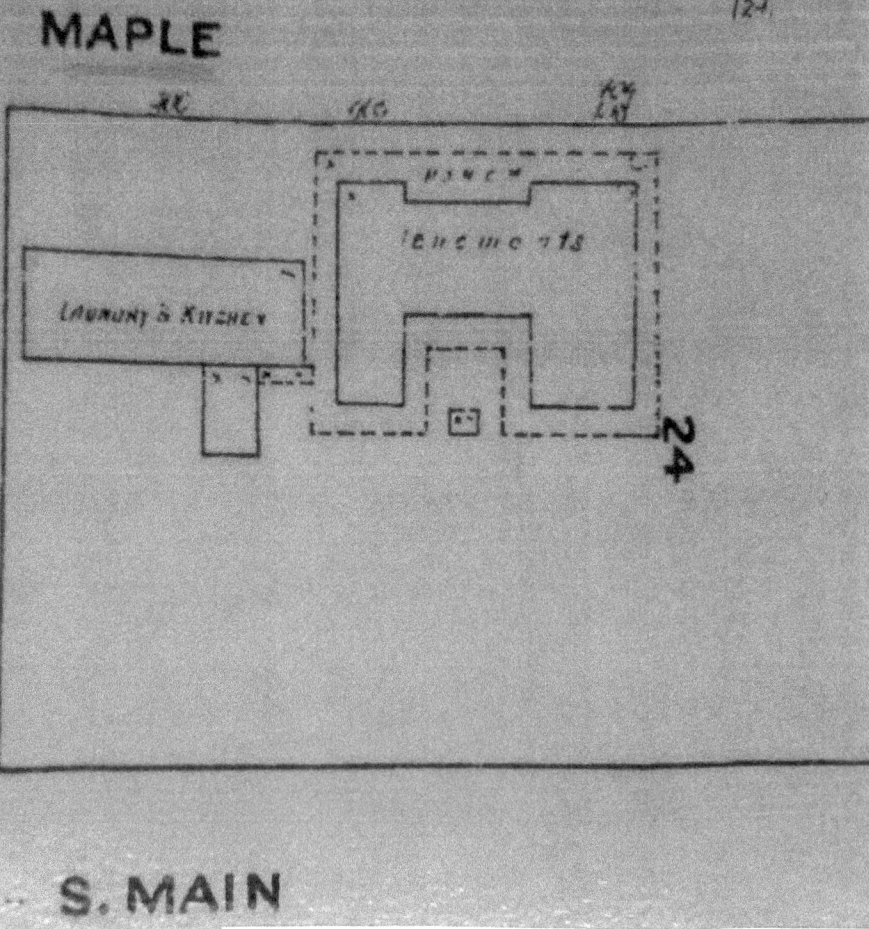

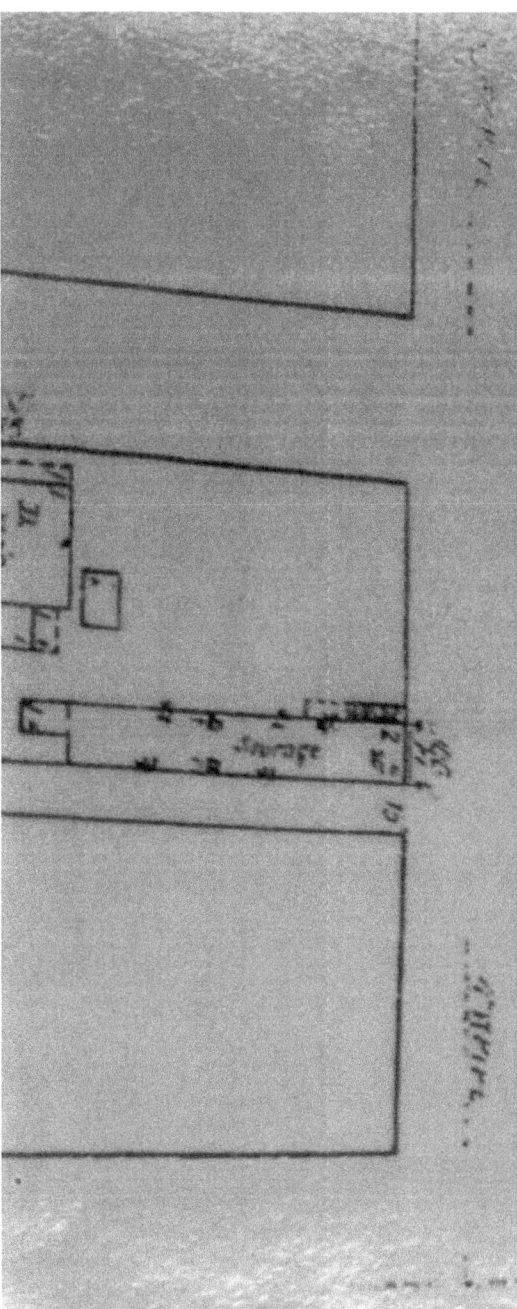

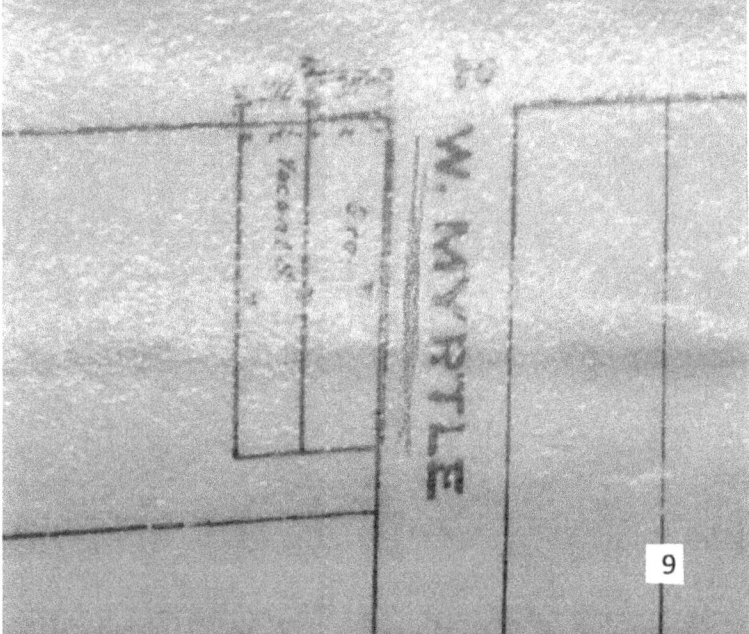

CENTRAL BAPTIST CHURCH

MAPLE

Laundry & Kitchen

Church

Tenements

18 A

24

S. MAIN

W. MYRTLE

9

CENTRAL BAPTIST CHURCH
Myrtle and Maple Streets
1904 - December 6, 1926

OUR THIRD AND CURRENT CHURCH BUILDING

Central Baptist Church has been a shining beacon to the people of Gainesville and Hall County for 133 years. When the church began as a mission, the community gave all they could and moved the ministry forward. Then the church was organized with 15 members and it continued to grow.

The difficult years during the depression were memorable. A few members rolled up their sleeves, worked hours for the benefit of church progress and outreach to the community and nation. The beautiful church structure that was completed in 1932 is a lasting legacy to these great church pioneers.

--In 1919, a decision was made to buy land on Main Street. Rev. Scott Patterson purchased the property because the church could not afford to buy it. We finally paid him on February 11, 1920.

--On June 7, 1925, the church voted to build a new church--Charles Edison drew up plans and presented them to the church and the church approved them.

--In August 1925, the foundation was laid.

--On December 2, 1925, the outside walls were coated with tar.

--The first meeting was held in the basement on the second Sunday in December 1926.

--In 1927, the WMU contributed $122 for three windows in the church. Rev R.D. Hawkins's name was placed on one.

--The first brick was laid on June 9, 1928.

--On October 20, 1929, the church authorized the trustees to borrow $10,000 from the Home Missions Board to complete the construction of the new building. (The loan was paid off in 1942.)

--In 1930, The WMU purchased for $275 the stain glass windows above the baptistery.

--DR. WILLIAM KEEL (1928-1934), was pastor when much of the work on the church took place.

PASTORS

J.L.R. Barrett

1891-1894

D.S. McCurry

1894-1895

W. J. Wooten

1896-1897

J.R. DeLong

1897-1898

James Austin Bell

1898-1899

Alexis Dawson Kendrick

1899-1900

John Cullen Otwell

1901-1905

Madison Monroe Riley

1905-1906

Charles Truman Brown

1907-1909

Addison Baxter Smith

1910-1911

Henry Franklin Wood

1911-1914

Joseph Anthony
Crumbley

1914-1916

11

L.L. Bennett

1916-1917

B.W. Mercier

1918-1919

Alonzo Scott Patterson

1919-1920

Roland W. Selman

1920-1922 & 1924-1925

John T. Grizzle

1922-1924

Augustus F. Smith

1926-1928

William A. Keel

1928-1934

K. Owen White

1934-1936

Warren Jeffrey Jones, Sr.

1937-1944

Raymond C. Moore

1944-1948

James W. McRay

1948-1956

W. Richard Bates

1956-1959

Evan Bishop Shivers

1959-1961

Charles Wesley Drake

1961-1968

HAROLD FREDERIC GREEN

1968-1978

TRUMAN C. SKAGGS

1979-1993

Larry C. Tomlin
1994-2001

Earl Pirkle
2002-2017

MIKE TAYLOR
2019

Pastors Who Have Served Central

J. L. R. Barrett	—	1891-1894	Roland W. Selman	—	1920-1922
D. S. McCurry	—	1894-1895	J. T. Grizzle	—	1922-1924
W. J. Wooten	—	1896-1897	Roland W. Selman	—	1924-1925
J. R. DeLong	—	1897-1898	A. F. Smith	—	1925-1928
J. A. Bell	—	1898-1899	William A. Keel	—	1928-1934
A. D. Kendrick	—	1899-1900	K. Owen White	—	1934-1936
J. C. Otwell	—	1901-1905	Warren Jeffrey Jones	—	1937-1944
M. M. Riley	—	1905-1906	Raymond C. Moore	—	1944-1948
C. T. Brown	—	1907-1909	James W. McRay	—	1948-1956
A. B. Smith	—	1910-1911	W. Richard Bates	—	1956-1959
H. F. Wood	—	1911-1914	E. B. Shivers	—	1959-1961
J. A. Crumley	—	1914-1916	Charles W. Drake	—	1961-1968
L. L. Bennett	—	1916-1917	Harold F. Green	—	1968-1978
B. W. Mercier	—	1918-1919	Truman C. Skaggs	—	1979-1993
A. Scott Patterson	—	1919-1920	Larry C. Tomlin	---	1994-2001
			EARL PIRKLE	—	2002-2017

13

STAFF

FIRST PAID STAFF

Secretary, Miss Willie Taylor

1939 ($20 per month) – May 1950

First MUSIC DIRECTOR

J. C. Otwell

(Find Otwell Sermon Notes on pages 53 and 54)

1896

CHURCH CHORISTER

John Egbert (J. E.) Owen

September 1910, to April 6, 1936

CHURCH CHORISTERS

Frank W. DeLong, September 2, 1936, August 4, 1937, and September 2, 1942, and in 1949, served as Assistant until Rev. Ken Sliger was called in 1950.

Marvin E. Lawson, was elected Chorister January 13, 1937, and in 1949, he served as codirector until Ken Sliger came. He served as Interim Music Director from September 4, 1952, until Homer Walker arrived in 1953.

M. P. Jones, was elected on September 8, 1943, and on October 2, 1946.

MUSIC MINISTERS

Minister of Music and Education, Rev. Kenneth Slinger, June 15, 1950, to October, 1951.

Clarence P. Cox, Minister of Music and Education, October 11, 1951, to August 1952.

Homer Henry Walker, Minister of Music and Education, 1953, 1954, 1955, to April 1,1956.

Dr. Scott Patterson, Interim Pastor, July 26, 1956, to October 21, 1956, and again from October 1959, to January 21, 1960.

STAFF

Bob Thompson, Interim Music, (When Dr. Scott Patterson was Interim
Pastor in 1956 and again in 1959, Bob confirmed this.).

FIRST MINISTER OF YOUTH

John Dalton, July 1, 1957, to December 1960.

Rev. Walter Blackwell, Interim Pastor, April 5, 1961, to August 1961.

Verne Taylor, Minister of Music and Youth, January 15, 1961, to July 21, 1961.

Dr. Kenneth Baumgardner, Music Interim, August 1963, to March 1964.

Eugene Griffith, Minister of Music and Youth, June 1, 1964, to November 8, 1967.

Earnest P. Mason (Ernie), Music Interim, November 15, 1967, to May 26, 1968.

Rev. R. W. Prevost, Interim Pastor, June 9, 1968, to October 1, 1968.

Dr. Kenneth Baumgardner, Music Interim, June 5, 1968, 1969, to March 29, 1970.

W. A. "Bud" Stengell, Jr., Minister of Music and Youth, March 16, 1970, to August
3, 1976.

Marvin Goodman, Minister of Education, July 1, 1972, to June 10, 1973.

George Collins, Minister of Music, August 7, 1977, to February 11, 1979.

Dr. J. T. Ford, Interim Pastor, January 1979, to August 1979.

Don Davis, Minister of Music, April 12, 1979, to July 1980.

Don Elrod, Interim Music and Youth, May 25, 1980, to June 29, 1980, then
Associate Pastor Of Outreach and Administrative Assistant, 1980, 1981, 1982,
and Associate Pastor from 1983, to February 12, 1984.

David McLendon, Minister of Education and Youth July 1980, to December 1983.

Larry Wilbur, Minister of Education and Youth, March 17, 1985, to December 28,
1986.

C. V. Smith, Interim Music, February 1984, to March 1985, Minister of Music,
March 1985, to February 1994.

Richard McWhite, Minster of Education and Youth, May 1, 1987, to January 4,
1991.

STAFF

Danny Newbern, Interim Youth Director, January 1991, to May 1992.

Matt Benson, Summer Youth Minister, June, to August 1992.

Dwight Oakes, Education and Youth Minister, September 1992, to August 1998.

Ron Barker, Interim Pastor, April 1993, to February 1994.

J. B. Graham, Interim Pastor, March, to October 1994.

James M. Worley, Interim Minister of Music, January, to July 1996.

Ellis Martin, Minister of Music, August 1996, to November 2005.

Robby Kerr, Minister of Youth, September 1998, to August 2001.

Dr. John Lee Taylor, Interim Pastor, October 2001, to June 2002.

Kevin Ingram, Interim Associate Pastor, November 2001, to November 2002.

Jason Harrison, Minister of Youth, September 12, 2003, to May 2004.

Eric Woods, Minister of Youth and Music, January 29, 2006,

to November 2006.

Eddie Simmons, Minister of Youth, Music, and Outreach, January 28, 2007.

He did not work with the youth after 2011. In April 2018, he left our

fellowship.

Bradley Woodruff, Director of Youth, 2011 to December 29, 2013.

Craig Broome, Minister of Youth, January 5, 2014, to December 14, 2017.

Jim Gittens, Interim Minister of Music, April 2018, to 2020.

Rev. Terry Rice, Interim Pastor, April 2018, to March 2019.

Don Elrod, Minister of Music, January 2020.

Boone Strickland, Associate Pastor, August 9, 2020, to present.

HISPANIC MISSION

Richard E. Richey – Hispanic Pastor – January 27, 1985 –

Full-time   August 1, 1987

PARTIAL LIST OF INDIVIDUALS WHO HAVE MADE
A CAREER IN CHRISTIAN SERVICE

The following is a partial list of persons who have entered full-time Christian service as a direct influence from Central Baptist Church.

J. C. Otwell shared his call to preach in November 1982.

Clinton Crow, ordained to the gospel ministry September 14, 1900.

J. M. Pethel, ordained to the gospel ministry January 6, 1916.

P. J. Porter, licensed to preach on September 30, 1925.

J. W. A. Mooney, ordained to the gospel ministry June 5, 1929.

John Hulsey ordained a deacon October 4, 1935, already an ordained
    Minister.

Carl Simpson, ordained to the gospel ministry in 1939.

Harvey Morrison, licensed August 7, 1940.

Dan D. Moore, licensed August 1, 1945.

Ben Hatfield, ordained to the gospel ministry December 19, 1943.

A. Miller, licensed August 1, 1948.

H. T. Jarrard, licensed September 29, 1948.

Lacy Oliver, licensed June 4, 1952.

Tommie Simpson, August 1952.
Kenneth Sliger, called to the gospel ministry in 1950.

Bobby Howard, licensed June 10, 1953; ordained March 1954.

Bob Thompson, in 1959 went to New Orleans Baptist Theological Seminary.

David Brown, ordained to the gospel ministry March 7, 1965, at the request
    of Antioch Baptist Church, Dahlonega.

Wilbur Peeples ordained to the gospel ministry July 11, 1965, at the request
    of Zion hill Baptist Church.

David "Butch" Jones shared his call to the ministry in 1976.

Mark Cochran, licensed August 1976.

Harvey Crumley, licensed August 1976.

Alan Shope, licensed August 1976.

Howard Martin, licensed August 1976.

Tommy Campbell, licensed on February 12, 1989, by the Church of Carrollton, Kentucky.

Alan Sutton, licensed to preach April 3, 1983.

Gary Linderman, voted to be licensed on April 18, 1984.

Phillip Garrett, licensed as a minister of the Gospel on February 27, 1985.

Mrs. Betty Hawkins Carpenter, career missionary to Liberia, West Africa.

Betty and John Mark Carpenter

Wilburn and Willie Peeples

MISSIONS STARTED AND/OR ASSISTED BY CENTRAL

Emmanuel Baptist Church, Gainesville

Established September 26, 1937, under the leadership of Dr. W. Jeffrey Jones.

Victory Baptist Church, Gainesville

Constituted November 22, 1959, as the Victory Cooperative Missionary Baptist Church, (formerly the Melrose Mission which began on July 1, 1952).

The Southern Baptist Church of Knoxville, Iowa

Summer of 1971, sponsored by Central through the Home Mission Board.

The church voted on October 3, 1971, to provide monthly support.

Summit Street Mission, 1973.

Calvary Baptist Church, Elko, Nevada, 1973.

Central Baptist Church, Elko, Nevada, 1973.

Emmanuel Baptist Church, Cour d'Alene, Idaho, August, 1974.

First Baptist Church Riverview, Michigan, 1972.

Arab Speaking Work in New England, 1970's.

HISPANIC MISSION 1985

Constituted in August 1991, as the First Hispanic Baptist Church of Gainesville.

BUILDINGS AND LOCATIONS

---Miss Amanda McCants' Schoolhouse on the corner of Chestnut and High Streets was used when the church began as a mission.

---The First Baptist Church gave a lot on Chestnut Street in 1891, to build a church. The lot was valued at $200. In the church minutes on April 28, 1891, the minutes recorded that the church received only one-half of the lot because they thought it was more than ample for their needs.

---The church moved in June of 1892 to the first "Real" church on Chestnut Street. In September 1900, half of Chestnut Street property was sold for $50.

---June 1, 1903, the church was destroyed by a tornado.

---July 1904, moved to Maple and Myrtle Streets. This church was used until 1926.

---Dr. Scott Patterson bought the property our church is built on in 1919 because the church could not afford to buy it. On February 11, 1920, the church was able to pay Dr. Patterson and secure the deed.

---On July 7, 1925, the church voted to build a new church house. The church was completed 1932.

---In 1950, plans were drawn for the J. L. R. Barrett Building, (location of Fellowship Hall).

---In 1960, the Shivers Building was begun, (children's building).

---In 1970, the Patterson Building was renovated, and the library expanded, (Bessie Drake Library).

---During the March 10, 1970, church conference, Dr. Harold F. Green presented the idea of naming two of our buildings to add dignity and description to these areas. A motion was made and seconded on the matter. In April 1970, the buildings were officially named.

BUILDINGS AND LOCATIONS

March 1890 – June 1892
Corner of High and
Chestnut Streets

Chestnut Street Mission
March 1890
Chestnut Street Baptist
Church
January 30, 1891

June 1892 – June 1, 1903
(This church was destroyed
by a tornado.)

From June, 1903, until 1904,
worship services were held
in Hobbs Chapel, a house located
on Summit Street.

Central Baptist Church
Myrtle and Maple Streets
1904 – December 5, 1926

CENTRAL BAPTIST CHURCH
785 Main Street
Gainesville, Georgia 30501

21

since 1889...

In the 1880's Gainesville and Hall County were known as a resort and recreation area. Tourists and visitors came from Alabama, Florida, Louisiana, Mississippi, North Carolina, and South Carolina. The people came to get away from the heat, humid weather, and diseases. Many families visited every summer to enjoy the water of the springs located in the area. They believed the water from the springs made them stronger and caused then to have better health. Some people came just to enjoy the mountain breezes.

Places were needed for the visitors and tourists to stay. The Arlington Hotel (later named the Dixie Hunt, now Hunt Tower) was completed in 1882 and was one of the finest buildings in Northeast Georgia. The Richmond House was built near the railroad. The Piedmont Hotel, a large wooden building, was in a park covering several acres and was about two hundred yards from the railroad depot. The Piedmont Hotel was built and run by General James Longstreet.

General Longstreet was a distinguished Civil war veteran who had fought with General Robert E. Lee. After the Civil War, General Longstreet retired and moved to Gainesville.

The Hudson House was built on the square. It was later named the Princeton Hotel (where Woolworth's has been). There were many houses, called boarding houses, where visitors could rent rooms.

Main Street. GAINESVILLE, Ga.

THIS IS FROM A POSTCARD PRINTED IN GERMANY IN 1910. A TROLLY IS RETURNING DOWN GREEN STREET AROUND THE ACADEMY STREET AREA.

BY 1877, A HORSE-DRAWN RAILROAD (STREET CAR) WAS OPERATING FROM THE SOUTHERN RAILROAD DEPOT, UP MAIN STREET, AND RIVERSIDE DRIVE TO THE CHATTAHOOCHEE PARK. ELECTRIC STREET CARS BEGAN RUN-NING JANUARY 21, 1903. THE TRACKS WERE TAKEN UP IN 1927. SOME TRACKS ARE TO BE SEEN TODAY!

GAINESVILLE, GA. Green Street

THE FIRST DECADE

1890-1900

"The Dream Begins"

The phrase "The Gay Nineties" evokes the atmosphere of being carefree, but to many citizens of Gainesville who lived through the panic of 1893 and the depression which followed, life was often anything but gay. Central was active during these years. A young church which began as a mission in March, 1890, and was constituted as a church on January 30, 1891, was trying to meet the needs of a group of citizens located on Chestnut Street in Gainesville, Georgia, and fulfill the dream of concerned men and women.

Gainesville was a growing town. There were two banks in town and many new buildings were constructed around the square to help meet the growing needs of the town. These included dry goods stores, drug stores, grocery stores, cotton and fertilizer dealers, hardware stores, cabinet shops, shoe makers, attorney and real estate offices, insurance agencies, soda fountains, and restaurants. Gainesville grew from a population of about 300 in 1872 to 4,000

in 1888.

During Central's first decade six pastors served Chestnut Street Baptist Church. At this time in church history many churches had an annual call for a pastor.

J. L. R. Barrett	1891-1894
D. S. McCurry	1894-1895
W. J. Wooten	1896-1897
J.R. DeLong	1897-1898
J. A. Bell	1898-1899
A. D. Kendricks	1899-1900

Following is a highlight of events of the first decade as gleaned from Central's church conference minutes.

---Chestnut Street Mission began in March 1890, assisted by First Baptist Church.

---Chestnut Street Baptist Church was organized on January 30, 1891, as a New Testament church. In conference on February 24, 1891, the minutes recorded that the First Baptist Church had contributed a lot valued at $200 for the purpose of building a house of worship.

----In April 1891, the church had its first revival (protracted meeting) with Dr. W. J. Wooten.

----The first baptisms took place on the first Sunday in June 1891, when William E. Bray and Dovie Coker were baptized.

----On July 5, 1891, the church received its first offering for Foreign Missions for a Southern Baptist missionary in China with sacrificial offering of $1.55. (This was five cents more than five cents for each member.)

----The first Building Committee report came on February 24, 1891, when the church recorded $247.15 saved for the purpose of building a house of worship plus $15.15 Pastor Barrett reported as having on hand.

----In September 1891, the church applied for admission into Chattahoochee Baptist Association. (Confirmed in business session on September 29, 1891.)

----September 29, 1891, the first deacons were ordained. They were J. W. Emmett and W.M. Hadaway.

----First Sunday, January 1892, the observance of the Lord's Supper took place.

----June 1892, the church moved into the first house of worship Chestnut Street.

 ----In October 1892, Pastor J. L. R. Barrett agreed to serve the church exclusively (full-time).

----First music director May 5, 1896, to September 8, 1899, was J. C. Otwell.

----December 4, 1898, the church voted to begin using offering envelopes. They were given January 1899. February 1899, the church decided to utilize literature for Sunday School.

THE SECOND DECADE

1900-1910

"The Difficult Dream"

Gainesville did not stop growing. By 1902 Gainesville was known as the metropolis of north Georgia and an excellent place to live. Gainesville had two electric plants, a water works system, a fire department, post office, modern city and county buildings, cement brick and stone sidewalks, beautiful streets, many churches, a telephone system, three banks, three brick plants, and two newspapers, the **Georgia Cracker** and the **Gainesville Eagle.**

There were many other businesses such as iron and machine shops, three cotton mills, a tannery, a shoe factory, lumber mills, livery stables, a bottling company, two railroads, and other stores of all descriptions around the square.

Gainesville had its first lights turned on in December 1902. The rural areas did not get electric lights until years later.

A tornado hit Gainesville on June 1, 1903. Many children died because there was no "child labor law", and they were hired to work in the mills. Two stories of the three-story building of Gainesville Mill were destroyed and many children were at work on these floors.

People from Atlanta and other cities came immediately by train to help. Many other cities helped the victims of the tornado by sending money.

In conference minutes during this decade and through 1920 the church was constantly investigating members for breaking the sabbath, drinking, heresy, swearing, and failing to attend church on a regular basis. Many apologized; others were "turned out" or excluded from the church.

Also, during this decade the church was led by J. C. Otwell through the devastating tornado which destroyed the church. The relocation and rebuilding of the church and a change in its name took place under his watch.

Four pastors served Central Baptist Church during the years 1900-1910.

J. C. Otwell   1900-1905

Dr. M. M. Riley   1905-1906

Charles T. Brown   1907-1909

A. B. Smith   1910-1911

In September 1900, part of the church property on Chestnut Street was sold for $50.

In November 1900, the church purchased one hymnbook with words and music and forty books with just words.

On Monday June 1, 1903, the church was destroyed by a tornado. On June 10, Brother B. Roberts presented a resolution that a new house of worship be built to replace the one destroyed by the tornado.

On July 8, 1903, the church voted to purchase property on the corner of Myrtle and Maple Streets. On July 10, the church organized a fundraising and rebuilding committee. Also in July, the church sold the remainder of its property on Chestnut Street.

On April 6, 1904, the church unanimously voted to change its name to Central Baptist Church.

The Woman's Missionary Union was organized in April 1904, with twenty-seven members. Mrs. V. A. Jones was the first president.

The congregation moved into its new church building in 1904. The church had used a home, "Hobbs' Chapel, located on Summit Street during the time the new church was being constructed. The church was wired for electricity in 1905, one of the first to be wired.

A Sunbeam Band was organized on January 28, 1907.

THE THIRD DECADE

1910-1920

"A Turbulent Dream"

The church struggled to exist during the third decade. The conference minutes noted attempts to encourage regular attendance on the part of its members. There was a preoccupation with church members reported for various sins and ensuing investigations. Money problems continued to plague the church. On September 30,1910, finances were so bad the church voted to cut to two Sunday Worship Services, and cut from $75 to $50 monthly.

----Gainesville continued to grow, and more working people built and moved to the south side of town.

Central had six pastors during its third decade.

A. B. Smith	1910-1911
Henry Franklin Wood	1911-1914
J. A. Crumbley	1914-1916
L. L. Bennett	1916-1917
B. W. Mercier	1918-1919
Dr. Scott Patterson	1919-1920

----In conference September 4, 1912, the pastor's salary was set at $600 per year.

----The April 1913, conference was dedicated to one of Central's most outstanding members and former Pastor, J. C. Otwell. He died on April 7, 1913, in Monroe, Georgia. Rev. Otwell was a Charter Member.

-----We are blessed to have many of his notes and sermons. They are housed in the History Center.

---- July 8, 1914, the church voted for Pastor J. A. Crumbley to take a vacation at will.

----On March 21, 1916, a committee was appointed to consider the advisability of erecting a new house of worship.

----In conference July 5, 1916, two events were recorded: That fellowship be withdrawn from a brother for unchristian conduct, and that this church adopt the common custom of Baptist churches of granting the pastor an annual vacation, and that the same be granted at this time.

----In November 1918, Dr. Scott Patterson was called as pastor. He was on furlough from being a missionary in Nigeria.

----In November 1919, a decision was made to buy land on Main Street, but the church had to decline because of the price. Dr. Patterson bought the property himself and later transferred the property to the church and was reimbursed for his expenses.

SPECIAL NOTE----by A. Scott Patterson   Oct. 22, 1956

In the Fall of the year 1918, A. Scott Patterson, a missionary to Africa, came to Gainesville and finding Central Baptist Church without a minister, gave to the church spiritual advice and leadership. The church was then small, weak and discouraged. It was located on a small lot, in an inadequate building on Maple St.

In the month of December 1919 Bro. Patterson bought the present church lot on Main Street and after raising the necessary money in the membership, on the 11th of February 1920, deeded said lot to Central Baptist Church.

All records of these transactions are recorded in the clerk's office in Hall County as follows:

    (1) John W. Whelchel to A. C. Wheeler—Dec. 3, 1919.
        (Recorded in Book 37, Page 341, July 16, 1920)

    (2) A. C. Wheeler to A. Scott Patterson—Dec. 16, 1919.
        (Recorded in Book 38, Page 89, July 16, 1920)

    (3) A. Scott Patterson to Central Baptist Church—Feb. 11, 1920.
        (Recorded in Book 38, Page 90, July 16, 1920)

In 1956, again the church being without a minister, A. Scott Patterson now near seventy two years old, rendered a similar service and during this period of service the lot on Bradford Street was purchased by the church. This ministry continued for a period of only five months.

A. Scott Patterson

THE FOURTH DECADE

1920-1930

"The Dream Expands"

For Central, this decade marked continuing church conferences in which members were brought before the church for disciplinary reasons. The church had financial problems, but still struggled to begin the building of our dear "old" church.

In the 1920's the downtown area changed. The streetcar tracks were taken up in July 1929 (The first cars were pulled by horses in 1874). In February 1928, the first automobile company, McConnell Auto Company was opened.

During the 1920-1930 decade six pastors led the church.

Dr. Scott Patterson	1919-April, 1920
Roland W. Selman	1920-1922
J. T. Grizzle	1922-1924
Roland W. Selman	1924-1925
A. F. Smith	1926-1928
Dr. William A Keel	1928-1934

On February 11, 1920, the church accepted the deed to a lot on Main Street from Dr. Scott Patterson and voted to write a resolution of thanks. (This is our current location.)

On April 12, 1920, the church voted to furnish the pastor a home and an annual salary of $1,500. On August 4, 1920, it was ordered that the building committee be instructed to complete the pastor's home as early as possible. The treasurer was authorized to insure the pastor's home for $3,000.

On January 5, 1921, it was approved that Bro. R. W. Selman be allowed to remove some trees from the lot near the home for the purpose of making a garden.

In the spring of 1923, the Woman's Missionary Union started a Building Fund and had a Christmas Bazaar to raise money.

On September 5, 1923, the church decided to sell its tent that had been used during the transition from Myrtle to Main Street. Dr. Patterson had used a tent to encourage members to hear him preach and enjoy the new lot. People began attending services and soon work was being done on the lot.

In April of 1924, it was recommended that the church choose nine active deacons, further that if nine could not be secured from those already ordained that the church ordain as many as necessary to have nine deacons. This was Central's first attempt at establishing a deacon body.

The church voted in conference on June 7, 1925, to build a new house of worship. On August 12, 1925, the Building Committee was authorized to purchase material for laying the foundation for the new church building.

In August 1925, the foundation was laid. On December 2, 1925, the outside walls were coated with tar.

In 1925, a member of the church reported that during a Sunday Morning service the roof was in such poor repair that when a rain shower occurred choir members had to hold umbrellas to stay dry.

In March 1926, the Myrtle Steet property was offered for sale for $4,000. It was sold on August 12, 1928, to the Salvation Army for $1,000.

On March 8, 1926, a petition was presented to pave Broad Street. On motion, the church voted not to pave the street.

The last church service was held in the church on Myrtle and Maple Streets on December 5, 1926. The church had been used for twenty-three years.

In 1927, the WMU contributed $122 for three windows in the church. Rev. R. D Hawkins' name was to be placed on one.

The first brick was laid on June 9, 1928. The basement was used for worship during part of the building time.

On October 20, 1929, the church authorized the trustees to borrow $10,000 from the Home Mission Board of the Southern Baptist Convention to complete the construction of the new building. The loan was paid off in 1941.

THE FIFTH DECADE

1930-1940

"The Dream Continues"

The Great Depression and the 1936 tornado were the hallmarks of Central's fifth decade, but the building program still continued.

In 1930, the Woman's Missionary Union purchased for $275 the stained-glass window above the baptistry.

On October 1, 1930, the church met and voted to organize a Brotherhood.

The church voted in February 1931, to buy 208 opera chairs from the State Theatre for the price of forty cents each for the growing Sunday School, and they are still in the balcony.

The 1931-32 budget was $5,600.

Dr. Keel was the first pastor to break the practice of an annual call.

On January 6, 1932, the church voted to raise money to pay off the remainder of the pews.

The 1935 budget was $5,200; the 1936 budget was $6,000; the 1937 budget was $7,000.

Three pastors served the church during these difficult times.

Dr. William A. Keel	1928-1934
Dr. K. O. White	1934-1936
Dr. W. Jeffrey Jones	1937-1944

Mrs. Ruby Maddox has told me of the times her father, Mr. Allison, worked on the church building. She said he was there when the foundation was laid and when the bricks were laid. She told me that when she and Mr. Burl got married tithing was one thing they started and never stopped. Ruby was active in the work of the church for many years. Ruby and Burl Maddox were the parents of Barbara Hall.

January 2004, Helen M. Martin

RUBY ALLISON MADDOX

One of Gainesville's greatest disasters happened on Monday, April 6, 1936. Fourteen city blocks were destroyed when a tornado swept through the city. More than 750 homes were demolished; 250 more were damaged, and the heart of the business area was torn to pieces. Property damage was estimated at more than thirteen million dollars, six million in the business section and seven million in the residential area. These statistics are on the computer and many places.

Many people were killed and injured. Approximately 227 people were killed, and 750 were seriously injured. People from Atlanta and other places came to help the residents of Gainesville. Everyone who lived in Gainesville worked together to rebuild the city.

After the April 6, 1936, tornado, Central was the only downtown church that remained totally unharmed. It was used as a first aid station.

---From the church minutes:

Sept. 30, 1936: following is a list of the names of our members who died during the church year (October 1935, to October 1, 1936), some of which were killed by the terrible tornado that devastated a large portion of Gainesville and vicinity on April 6. Our deceased members are Deacon A. E. Fuller, Mrs. Jane Latimer, Deacon J. E. Owen, Mrs. Eula Dooley, Mrs. Flora Burtz, Mrs. Cliff Mayes, Miss Helen Burtz, Mr. George Whitmire, Mrs. Jennie Hulsey, and Mrs. E. H. Brown.

The April 1936, church minutes reported no conference because of the tornado.

On March 3, 1937, upon the recommendation of the Deacons, the members voted to contribute to the churches suffering heavy losses in the recent floods in the Ohio and Mississippi River Valley.

The 1939 budget was $16,000, and in June of that year the pastoral annuity plan was begun.

In August of 1939 the first youth revival was held.

THE SIXTH DECADE

1940-1950

'The Dream Flourishes"

World War II brought many changes to Gainesville during the early 1940's. The government issued stamps for sugar, gas, and meat. If you cooked ham for one meal you had to cook fatback for the next because it took so many stamps to buy good meat. Also, stamps were needed to buy shoes, and only enough were issued for the number of people in a family. Stamps had to be used to purchase shortening.

A family received only enough gas stamps to cover the distance from home to work. Many people bought gas stamps on the black market. Carpooling

was necessary.

The economy, however, grew rapidly, and the chicken industry became the major industry. Fewer people in the area continued to farm. Many of Gainesville's young men were drafted into the military service.

There were three pastors who served Central during this time.

Dr. W. Jeffrey Jones	1937-1944
Dr. Raymond C. Moore	1944-1948
Dr. James McRay	1948-1957

In March 1940, the church voted to publish a church paper, "The Clarion". Dr. W. Jeffrey Jones was pastor.

In August 1940, the average church attendance was 160. The 1940 budget was $10,000.

In 1941, a radio ministry on WGGA began under Dr. Jones' leadership, cost of $75 per month.

In April 1942, the church gathered to pay off the long-standing debt to the Home Mission Board. The money had been borrowed in 1929.

On March 7, 1945, the church voted to purchase choir robes. On August 1, the church voted to order an electric Hammond organ at a cost of approximately $1700.

On October 31, 1945, the church in conference adopted the recommendation of the deacons to give special recognition to our returned veterans.

On November 19, 1945, a recommendation from the deacons was ratified that a committee be appointed by the Chairman of the Board to frame by-laws for the church.

The 1947 budget was $14,000.

On April 2, 1947, the church constitution and by-laws were read, explained, and approved.

Dr. James McRay was called as pastor on April 10, 1948.

Under Dr. McRay's dynamic leadership, Central broke all existing attendance records. The church was making a new page in history.

On August 1, 1948, the church voted to organize Men's Brotherhood. Also, 1948, the **Christian Index** was included in the church budget for each church member.

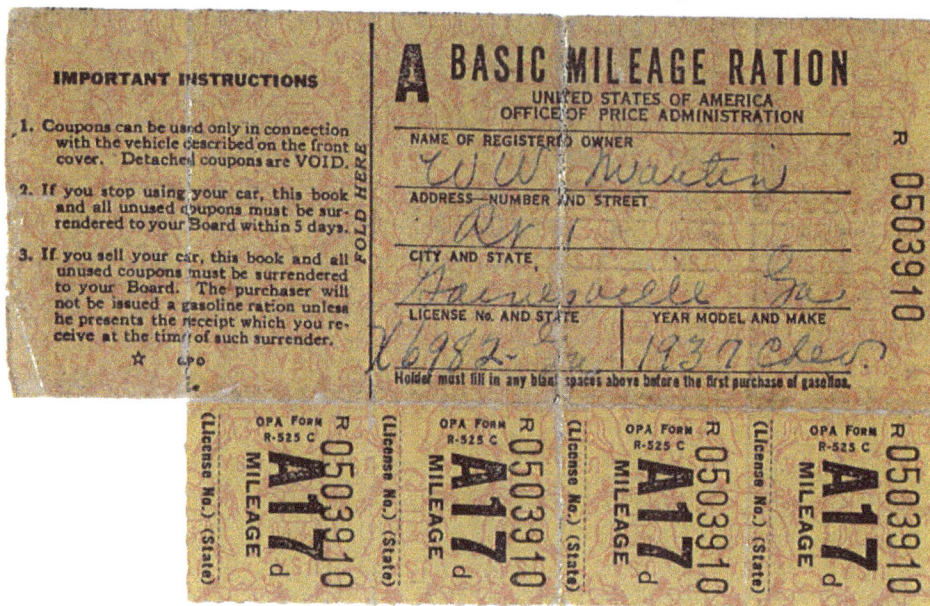

The gasoline stamps are samples that belonged to my father, William Walker Martin, from his WWII collection. Money was no good without enough stamps to make a purchase.   Helen M. Martin

THE SEVENTH DECADE

1950-1960

"The Thriving Dream"

Central Baptist Church enjoyed a great period of growth during the late 1940's and the early part of the 1950's. In October of 1950 Central averaged 336 in Training Union. In 1954 and 1955 all attendance records were broken.

Lake Sidney Lanier was constructed by the Army Corps of Engineers to serve as a source of electrical energy for the growing area. The lake opened in 1958. Since its opening, Gainesville has become an even more important and desirable place to live. Lake Lanier has an underwater acreage in Hall County of 47,000 acres. About twenty percent of Gainesville (1,316 acres) is under water.

Lake Lanier is an important resource in our area. The water is used to supply fresh water and electricity to Gainesville and many other cities. It is also used by millions of people each year for recreation.

Gainesville has changed a great deal since the 1950's. The large white building on the corner of Main and Washington Streets, the same side the Hall County Library is on was the Princeton Hotel. It was torn down and a new building constructed. Woolworth's was in the building in recent years, and a dress shop is currently there now. It is often sad to watch a city change, but as growth takes place, changes must occur.

Three pastors served during this decade.

Dr. James McRay	1948-1956
Dr. W. Richard Bates	1956-1959
Dr. E. B. Shivers, Sr.	1959-1961

The 1950 budget was $40,460. In October 1950, Training Union averaged 336 in attendance, and on November 29, 1950, the church voted to incorporate. Also, the Barrett Building was begun in June of 1950.

On January 10, 1951, the church voted to borrow $25,000 to finish the Barrett Building. In March of the next year, a decision was made to send "The Clarion" into every home.

The average attendance in Training Union in 1951 was 400. Later that spring property was purchased for the Melrose Chapel. Late in 1952, a decision was made to purchase a new pastorium since the one was needed for Sunday School space. By the end of that year Sunday School enrollment was 1,855.

In 1953, the church voted to redecorate the auditorium and landscape the grounds at a cost of $17,000. On July 1 of that year the church bought a house at 354 Green Street for $16,000 and sold it in November at a loss. Plans were made to build a new pastorium. Property was purchased at 1259 Burns Drive for $2,500, and a pastorium was built.

The 1954 budget was $93,750. During the 1954-55 church year, all church records were broken under the leadership of Dr. James McRay.

On Monday, March 5, 1956, a motion was made in deacons meeting to "sponsor" a new church at a location to be decided upon later and that Central property be mortgaged to meet the initial building program. On March 7, the motion failed in a church session.

During October 1957, additional land was purchased at the corner of Bradford and Summit Streets for $10,000.

On November 16, 1959, the Deacons recommended and approved the authorization of the Melrose Mission to be constituted into the Victory Cooperative Missionary Baptist Church on November 22 ,1959.

THE EIGHTH DECADE

1960-1970

"The Educational Dream"

During this decade much attention was given to the construction of an educational facility and the addition of a number of library books. Mrs. Charles (Bessie) Drake was largely responsible of the expansion of the library.

In May 1960, plans were made for the construction of the Shivers Building with the cost not to exceed $85,000. The building was to have two floors and contain 8,400 square feet of floor space.

The 1961 budget was $88,565. In March of that year Dr. Shivers began Easter Sunrise services at Memorial Park. It was about this time that the community around the church began to deteriorate.

There were pastors who served Central during this decade.

E. B. Shivers	1959-1961
Charles W. Drake	1961-1968
Harold F. Green	1968-1978

Wednesday evening Family Suppers began in January 1962. In June the Boyd property on Summit Street was purchased for $10,000.

The 1963 year began with 598 present in Sunday School and 179 in Training Union. Central was beginning to know what it means to be inner city. Dr. Drake fought this battle during his entire ministry at Central. The area was becoming more industrialized and people were moving from the city.

On April 15, 1964, the deacons recommended that the church accept pulpit furniture and choir chairs from an anonymous donor with grateful hearts and appreciation without cost to the church.

Pastor Charles Drake participated in an Evangelistic Crusade in Jamacia March 7-21, 1965.

From June 16, 1965, church minutes, Brother George Wiley read the following Deacon recommendations:

1. The Pastor and Music Director be sent to the Baptist World Alliance meeting as our representatives. Mr. and Mrs. L. N. Adams are also to attend.
2. The Deacon Board recommends that members of different races be accepted to be a part of us if they come to worship.
3. The Pastor read a letter from Zion Hill Baptist Church requesting ordination of Wilbur E. Peeples as a minister. The motion was made and seconded that we proceed with the ordination on July 11, at 3 p.m. and the service to be held at Central Baptist Church.

Mrs. Raymond Moore, pastor's wife in the 1940's began the library, and it was expanded by Mrs. Charles Drake, pastor's wife, in the 1960's.

During a church conference held December 8, 1965, the library report showed 740 books, with several books not yet processed. Mrs. Bessie (Charles) Drake urged everyone to take advantage of the library by reading a book a month.

In 1967 a large bus was purchased.

During 1968 only seven people were won to Christ. Every conceivable method of outreach was used. Also in 1968, many members called for their letters. An average of one letter per day was granted for a period of six months.

Dr. Charles Drake resigned early in 1968 to accept another pastorate. Rev. R. W. Prevost, a retired minister from Tennessee, served as interim pastor. Dr. Harold F. Green came on October 1, 1968, just thirty-six years old, to serve as pastor. Dr. Baumgardner music professor from Brenau College was the interim minister of music from May 1968, until Easter, 1970. W. A. "Bud" Stengell, Jr. became Minister of Music at Easter in 1970.

After Dr. Green's arrival, the Patterson Building's first floor was renovated, new office spaces were built, and the library facility was expanded. With Dr. Greene's dynamic personality and outstanding preaching, the church began a period of growth that went into the 1970's.

THE NINTH DECADE

1970-1980

"The Rebuilding Dream"

This decade was one of both growth and setback. During Dr. Harold Green's ministry, the church grew in worship attendance, and it became necessary to hold two worship services each Sunday.

Gainesville took on a new face during the decade of the 1970's. New industries moved to Gainesville; the population in the 1970 census was 15,459 in Gainesville and 59,405, in Hall County. A great deal of reconstruction was begun in the downtown area and the community around our church completely changed.

March 10, 1970, Dr. Green presented the idea of naming two of our un-named buildings. A vote was taken and in April 1970, all buildings were officially named. The educational facility just beyond the sanctuary is called the Patterson Building named in honor of Dr. Scott Patterson who served as pastor from 1919 to 1920 and again as interim 1956 and 1959. The J. L. R. Barrett was named in honor of our first pastor, and is where the Fellowship Hall is located and serves as a Sunday School Facility. The Shivers Building, the children's facility, was named in honor of Dr. Evan Bishop Shivers who was pastor in 1959, to 1961. He was pastor at the time the building was under construction.

The 1971 budget was $132, 606. In January of that year, the 80th Anniversary of the church was celebrated. There were 1,300 people present.

On December 3, 1972, Bob Herington, "Chaplain on Bourbon Steet," in New Orleans preached with 4,500 in attendance. There were 139 decisions made for Christ. Dr. K. Owen spoke at the 82nd Anniversary in 1973. The 1973 budget was set at $160,309, and during the 1973-1974 church year two morning services were held.

In 1974, Dr. Green authored a book entitled, NOT MADE FOR DEFEAT. The book highlighted all pastors with a picture and brief biography. It also captured events and special activities in the church's eighty year history.

Dr. Harold F. Green resigned as pastor on November 5, 1978. With the resignation of Dr. Green, church attendance and membership declined. There was a total of 79 in Vacation Bible School in June 1979.

Dr. J. T. Ford served as interim pastor from January to August 1979. Truman Skaggs was called to serve the church in September 1979, and brought healing and non-stop enthusiasm to our church.

There were two pastors who served during this this decade.

Harold F. Green	1968-1978
Truman C. Skaggs	1979-1993

Truman Collier Skaggs became the twenty-ninth pastor in September 1979. The 1979 budget was $112,331. The Lottie Moon Christmas Offering totaled $3,353.

DR. GREEN

NOT
MADE
FOR DEFEAT...

The History Of The Central Baptist Church
from 1890—1974

by
Harold Frederic Green

THE TENTH DECADE

1980-1990

"The Renovating Dream"

Under the leadership of Pastor Truman C. Skaggs the balcony was reinforced to make it safe for years to come. Also, during this decade major renovations of all our facilities were made, costing more than $400,000.

Dr. W. Jeffery Jones was recognized as Central's Pastor Emeritus on November 13, 1983. This action was proposed by Rev. Truman C. Skaggs. A special parking spot was set aside for Dr. Jones.

In 1985, the church initiated a ministry among the Hispanics of Gainesville and Hall County. This work had the objective of reaching Hispanics for Christ and seeing them established in their own local church. The effort was led by Pastor Skaggs and Rev. Dick Richey, the first pastor of the new fellowship. More than $80,000 was on hand for the purchase of property and buildings for this ministry.

Many dynamic speakers have come to Central; among them have been four former presidents of the Southern Baptist Convention: Dr. K. Owen White, Dr. Herschel H. Hobbs, Dr. J. D. Grey, and Dr. Charles Stanley. Others include Dr. Jim Henry, Dr. Harold Skaggs, Dr. Robert White, Dr. C. Ford Duesner, and Dr. Harold L. Green.

Mission giving grew with the largest Lottie Moon Christmas Offering ever given of $11,099 in 1988.

Many people came to know the Lord as Savior. There were 234 additions to the church by baptism during this decade.

In the Woman's Missionary Union monthly ministry to the women of the Hall County Correctional Institution, there have been 334 professions of faith since 1985.

Through Pastor Skaggs' leadership, Central raised and spent over $400,000 in a major renovation program which included the Barrett, Shivers, and Patterson buildings. He always insisted that the church stay out of debt in order that we could broaden our ministry when television became available, reasoning that the church that was debt-free could afford a television ministry.

Central launched a television ministry on WNGM-TV, Channel 34, August 13, 1989. E. Lanier Finch, president of WNGM Television, presented to Pastor Truman C. Skaggs during a morning worship service an engraved citation for his leadership in pioneering religions television in the Gainesville/Hall County area.

WNGM-TV CHANNEL 34 — ATHENS/GAINESVILLE
PRESENTS OUR JULY 1 PATRIOTIC WORSHIP SERVICE
AS A SPECIAL JULY 4th AT 11 a.m.

One pastor served during this decade.
Truman C. Skaggs   1979-1993

THE ELEVENTH DECADE

1990-2000

"The Dream Lives on"

The decade of the 1990's was marked by both joy and great disappointment. Pastor Truman C. Skaggs, Central's longest serving pastor retired in 1993.

The 1990 budget was $299,904; the Lottie Moon Christmas offering was $7,461.75.

The television ministry became an asset to the church and the spreading of the gospel to the Northeast Georgia area. It was unusual for Pastor Truman and Dorothy to eat out or visit without someone recognizing them because of the television ministry on WNGM--TV, Channel 34.

During January 25, 26, 27, 1991, Central Baptist celebrated its 100th anniversary. What a time of joy and praise to God!

The First Hispanic Baptist Church of Gainesville sponsored by Central was opened on September 29, 1991. This helped in leading the people of Central to realize that the community and world was rapidly and continually changing.

The theme for Central during the ministry of Truman C. Skaggs was, "The Church of The Open Door-The Church with A Great Sunday Night Service." A Sunday night treat was the performance of the Blue Flames Men's Choir under the direction of Mr. Waldon.

An ill-fated interim ministry created a breach of fellowship from the time of Pastor Skaggs' retirement in 1993 until it ended in February 1994. Dr. J. B. Graham came as Interim Pastor from March until October 1994. Dr. Graham came with a "sweet" spirit and helped in healing the wounds of the church.

Dr. Larry Tomlin and his wife Becky served the church from January 1994, until January 2001. During his ministry, the church entered into an Atrium-elevator building program and was finally completed in 2001.

The Goldie Davis Memorial Heritage Facility was dedicated on January 25, 1996. This was created to house historical documents and church history. All historical material gleaned from all over the church were catalogued and moved to a designated area that became the GOLDIE DAVIS MEMORIAL CENTER.

A new Rogers 835B organ was dedicated on Sunday, September 20, 1998.

Two pastors served Central during this decade.

Truman Skaggs	1979-1993
Larry C. Tomlin	1994-2001

Goldie Davis was a petite and uniquely refined Southern Christian lady with a fine mind and loving heart. She had an effervescent personality that blessed her family and Central Baptist Church. She was a lady of poise, great talent and grace with a pleasing, compassionate voice that drew people to her. Goldie was always a friend to children, and her pastor's trusted confident.
Truman C. Skaggs
January 25, 1996

Mrs. Goldie Davis

From January, 1996, until today our history memorable and collection has grown as church members and friends have shared treasures they had tucked away. We outgrew the original room in the basement. During the fall of 2003, the church generously gave us a larger space on the second floor in the Patterson Building above the church offices.

Please take time if you have not visited the many treasures of our church to learn more about Central's past, present, and future dreams for fellowship and growth.

Over the years, Truman C. Skaggs had an extensive Christian Library. We are blessed to have been given Rev. Skaggs' Library by his son, Jody D. Skaggs. What a treasure this will be for Central, and it is housed in our basement.

TWELVETH DECADE

2000-2010

"A Dream for Spiritual Growth"

The new century began with Central's determination to move forward as the world was in the midst of fears and sometimes panic over threats of technological blackouts and threats of terror. The face of the world changed and no longer could we be content to look only at the world around us. The church was in a constantly changing ideology of socialism, and the world was engaged in a costly war in the middle east.

The church continued its struggle to complete the Atrium-*Elevator* project and found itself once again without a pastor. Dr. John Lee Taylor, retired pastor, First Baptist Church, Gainesville, Georgia, accepted Central's call in September 2001 to serve as interim pastor. Dr. Taylor and his wife, Delores led us as we struggled to stay afloat both spiritually and physically.

The Taylor's served until 2002 and decided to leave to make way for our new Pastor Earl Pirkle who came to us with his wife Sherry and daughters, Hannah and Mary Elizabeth.

Under Pastor Earl Pirkle's leadership the debt of the Atrium-Elevator Project was paid off. The debt decreased from $262,000 in January 2003, to $130,000 in January 2004. The final payment of $66, 319.45 came on March 3, 2006.

The Goldie Davis Memorial Heritage Facility dedicated in January 1996, occupied a new location on the second floor in the main church building. It was officially named and rededicated on January 25, 2004.

The Bertie McKinstry money was used for the renovation of the Shiver's Building. The Shiver's Building was built in 1960 and needed much renovation.

Two pastors served during this decade.

Larry C. Tomlin	1994-2001
Earl Pirkle	2002-2017

THIRTEENTH DECADE

2010-2020

"A Time of Trial and Redemption"

Over the years we have had growth and losses, but God has led us to always move forward in his name. When it seemed like we could not go down further, we have built up again. We have been able to pay our debts and keep the lights burning.

The "Cushion" project was spearheaded by the Stewardship Committee to help purchase new cushions for the pews in the Sanctuary. We raised enough to help in the cushion construction (the second phase of the project) with a theme first presented in the 1920's and 1930's when money was truly tight. Mrs. E. A. Burchfield embroidered the name of all who gave a dime toward the purchase of the beautiful baptismal window. The cost was $275. A 112-year-old quilt was used to stitch, by Betty Heathman and Helen Martin, the name or family who gave $100 toward the completion of new cushions. God blessed us with about $6,000.

At this point in our history, it is important to add a commentary written by Mrs. Jan Cobb who very ably chaired the Stewardship Committee through the Stained-Glass Window and the New Cushion Projects.

"I became Chairman of the Stewardship Committee for the 2014 year (beginning September 2013 thru September 2014.) Members were Marie Buffington, Carole Carter, Sue Martin, Betty Rooks, and Jim Delay, Treasurer; Ex Officio member was T. C. Reynolds. Pastor Earl Pirkle always sat in on the meeting. At the end of 2013 and in 2014, the church was struggling with needing many repairs, mold, mildew, and leaking roof and heat (radiator) were issues. I was told by Mary Ann Lee on many occasions we were not able to pay the pastor, her nor the musicians. We, the committee, presented the "Window" Project to membership and former members. That was to place names of classes or individuals on windows like the other marked windows throughout the Sanctuary and other places in the church. All were in agreement to pursue the project. The money was to be used by the Building and Grounds Committee for much needed repairs. The church was able to raise more than $70,000, in offerings dedicating some of the stained-glass windows that remained unmarked to current family, friend and members of our church." by Mrs. Jan Alton Cobb.

Mr. Craig Broome, our Minister of Youth, resigned on December 14, 2017, after serving from 2014. Mr. Eddie Simmons, Minister of Music, served from January 28, 2007, until April 2018. Then, when Pastor Earl Pirkle resigned the entire leadership turned over.

Pastor Earl Pirkle resigned as on December 17, 2017. He served from 2002 until his resignation. The membership accepted his departure with some degree of acceptance and reservation. We struggled for some months with different guest preachers. We were blessed with the arrival of our Interim Pastor, Rev. Terry Rice, in April 2018,until March 2019. He as a very good preacher with a "pastor's heart". We had an increase in Sunday School and preaching attendance. For a minister, he was a "better than average" cook and brought delicious dishes on Wednesday nights. We continued to have good Sunday School attendance with great Sunday School Teachers and well-attended Vacation Bible Schools.

Our Pastor Search Committee served faithfully for many, many, months searching for God's man to lead our church. On March 25, 2019, good news arrived. Rev. Mike Taylor and his wife Allison joined our fellowship. We have had many baptisms and new members have joined.

On the last Sunday in January 2020, we celebrated 130 years of service to the Lord, and we continue to reach out to our community and beyond.

1890 – 2020

Marking the 130th Anniversary of

CENTRAL BAPTIST CHURCH

785 Main Street

Gainesville, Georgia 30501

September 9, 2020

PRESENTED BY:

Joseph Royall Chapter (GA27)
Colonial Dames XVII Century

2020-PRESENT

"Central Baptist Church Post COVID Season"

The Central Baptist Church family greeted 2020 with great fanfare by celebrating our 130-year anniversary on January 26. The worship service was well attended, and a great feast was provided afterwards in the church fellowship hall. Little did we know of the dramatic changes to church life and American culture just ahead due to a pandemic called "coronavirus or COVID-19.

Georgia's governor ordered all citizens to "shelter in place" or stay home on Friday, March 13, 2020, with exceptions allowed only for "essential workers." As a result, the Central Baptist family did not meet at the church facility for Sunday School or worship on Sunday, March 15, 2020. It was the first of three (to date) extended interruptions to church life we experienced due to the pandemic COVID virus. Other interruptions from December 2020 – February 2021; and then again in July of 2022 when worship was cancelled to a wave of illnesses spreading among the church families.

Worship resumed in June of 2020. At first, we had no singing (to reduce airborne germs). Instead, Rev. Boone Strickland taught his Sunday School lesson from the pulpit and Pastor Taylor preached. Our instrumentalists Sue Tyner and John Hulsey played special music for these "bare-bones" services. By August of 2020, we returned to full S. S. and Worship with singing once again. Masks were distributed, every other pew was taped off to ensure 6 feet distances between non-family attenders, and plenty of hand sanitizer was provided. Matt Trawick and his cleaning crew sanitized the auditorium and Sunday School classes after each use. To minimize "touching", worship bulletins were no longer distributed and offering plates were no longer passed. Instead, one plate was provided on a pedestal adjacent to the Lord's table.

In the meantime, many adaptations sustained our communications and church family life, including the following steps:

The introduction of parking lot worship. The church purchased low-frequency transmitter, allowing us to broadcast a quarter mile in any direction from the church at 88.1 FM. Dozens of cars gathered in the Bradford Street parking lot to listen to the broadcast and wave at one another. Those in attendance were forbidden to get out of their vehicles to greet one another, and even told to refrain from lowering car windows.

Pastor Mike launched daily Bible devotions and prayer time on Monday, March 16, 2020, and has continued since then. The church invested in new cameras, and with Matt Trawick as media director, Central Baptist begin flooding social media with video messages.

Deacons began meeting every Monday for conference calls during which prayer requests were exchanged and church business was conducted over the telephone.

Looking back over 2.5 years of fighting COVID-19, the average church Sunday School and worship attendances suffered with as much as 20-25% decline. Slowly but surely, the church family is being strengthened by the reception of 40 new members since March 2019: half of them joining since the onset of the COVID pandemic.

The Lord tremendously blessed the Central Baptist family with a financial miracle during the seasons of not meeting. Several years ago the church struggled to pay bills and staff. However, total designated and general fund giving topped $450,000 for the year 2021, nearly doubling donations in 2019. The turnabout is partly due to careful management of church offerings and making amends to neglected accounting practices of the past. Many Ann Lee was sentenced to ten years of probation December 28, 2021, for her role in the diversion of church funds during her employment and the court ordered restitution of over $56,000. The investigation remains open with Gainesville police as of this date and an explanation of what happened to the remaining $200,000+ still missing. Central Baptist continues our "trek" of service to the Lord, believing we're "Not Made for Defeat!"

From Pastor Mike

Mike & Allison

Work of Presbytery.

Gainesville, Ga., Jan. 30, 1891.

According to previous arrangement a Presbytery, consisting of Revs. A. Van Hoose, F. C. McConnell and J. L. R. Barrett, met for the purpose of constituting a Baptist Church on Chestnut Street, in the school house of Sister Amanda McCants.

On motion Rev. A. Van Hoose was elected Chairman, and Rev. J. L. R. Barrett Secretary.

The following brethren and sisters presented letters and were received; 1. Bro. W. M. Hadaway, 2. Sister Ella Hadaway, 3. Bro. J. C. Otwell, 4. Bro. J. L. R. Barrett, (minister); 5. Sister G. W. Hicks, 6. Bro. W. M. Coker, (licensed minister); 7. Sister Coker, 8, and daughter, 9 Sister Lou Moore, 10. Bro. S. R. Tally, 11. Sister Tally, 12. Sister Elizabeth Coker, 13. Bro. W. P. Pirkle, 14. Sister Nancy N. Pirkle, 15. Sister Lucinda Moore. (W. H. Stewart?)

"Articles of Faith," "Church Order," and "Church Covenant" having been read and accepted, the church was declared a regularly constituted Baptist Church.

1891. *Names of Members.*

Jan 30. 1 W. M. Hadaway,

" " 2 Ella Hadaway,

" " 3 J. C. Otwell,

" " 4 J. L. R. Barrett (minister)

" " 5 Hicks.

" " 6 W. M. Coker. (licensed minister)

" " 7 Coker.

" " 8 Coker.

" " 9 Lou. Moore.

" " 10 S. R. Tally,

" " 11 Tally,

" " 12 Elizabeth Coker,

" " 13 W. P. Pirkle,

" " 14 N. N. Pirkle,

" " 15 Lucinda Moore.

The above are names of the "Charter" members of this church, or the ones went into it the day of its organization, and the order in which they came before the Presbytery.

W. H. Stewart was one of the Charter Members of Central. This was confirmed and recorded in the Church Minute Book. He was active in many church activities. Records confirm he was on the Building Committee in 1925 and served as a Trustee at the same time. He was present when the note was presented to the church showing the money borrowed from the Home Mission Board was paid in full. He died in 1965 after service to our church from 1891 until 1965.   #6   W. H. STEWART

John Cullen Otwell

1901-1905

AFTER 5 DAYS RETURN TO
J. C. OTWELL
BAPTIST MINISTER
GAINESVILLE, GEORGIA

Revival Sermons –

The Hypocrite
Mark 11.14 – 12–14.
Returning from Bethany
early Jesus is hungry
Possibly no food when
He spent the night.
He naturally looks
out for food
A few dates, figs, or piece
of bread plenty for an
Oriental's dinner
He sees at a distance
He sees a fig tree
Its rich leaves indi-
cated fruit.
There was a chance
to find either a late
or early supply –
There was nothing –
but leaves.
Then He denounces
the tree –
Teaching thereby a
great lesson

J. C. Otwell, our seventh pastor, was the Editor of the Gainesville Eagle, and an outstanding member of our community. He was active in the building of our first church. In our first Church Minute Book, you will see some beautiful penmanship he left our church. It is indeed a treasure and joy to read.

He accepted a call into the ministry in 1892, and became a Circuit Rider for other churches. He rode his horse, and in order to protect his sermon notes he carefully tucked them in his vest pocket on small pieces of paper.

<u>Elijah and the Prophets of Baal.</u>

<u>I Kings</u> <u>18. 30-38.</u>   [<u>Bethel Beth.</u>

<u>Prophets of Baal very much excited.</u>

They prayed regardless of law and order. <u>To no Gods</u>!!

<u>From</u> morning till noon – a long time,

<u>No answer from Baal, of course.</u>

<u>Time for the</u> evening sacrifice –
(Repairs altar.)

<u>Elijah proceeded obediently – lawfully.</u>

<u>Elijah was prepared – he prepared.</u>!

<u>Getting</u> every thing ready is necessary.

<u>Prayed at the time prescribed –</u>

<u>As a reason</u> he should be heard he
had done according to <u>God's Word.</u>

<u>God answered</u> while he was praying.

<u>He accomplished much – so may we.</u>

<u>If we are ready – and willing.</u>

Your Historian, Helen, was given J. C. Otwell's sermon notes by a family

member of Brother Otwell. We are blessed to have them, and they are

housed in the Goldie Davis Memorial Heritage Center.

An Important Statement Dr. Keel~1929 Helped the Trustees Draft~

Dr. William A. Keel served as our pastor from 1928, to 1934. He became the building pastor of the new church. He was also responsible for breaking the tradition of an annual call.

Dr. Keel spearheaded the development of a statement delivered by the trustees to execute and deliver to said church, in its corporate capacity resulting from the registration of its name, style, objects and names of its trustees. It was housed in the office of the Superior Court of Hall County, Georgia, October 21, 1929.

324

FROM CENTRAL'S CONFERENCE MINUTES, NOVEMBER 3, 1929.

Resolved by the Central Baptist Church of Gainesville Georgia, in regular church conference assembled, on this November 3rd, 1929, that said church, by its trustees B.H. Moore, W.B. Reed and Charles E. Eidson, execute and deliver to said church, in its corporate capacity resulting from the registration of its name, style, objects and names of its Trustees in the office of the Clerk of the Superior Court of Hall County, Georgia, on October 21, 1929, a Warranty deed to the property hereinafter described; said deed to be executed and delivered for the purpose of conveying said property from said Church in its capacity as it existed prior to said registration, to itself, in its corporate capacity resulting from said registration; said property being described as follows:

55

All that tract or parcel of land lying and being in the City of Gainesville, Hall County, Georgia, beginning at the corner of Main Street and High Street, and running north along said Main Street a distance of one hundred twenty-two (122) feet and four (4) inches to the Central Baptist Church Pastorium Property; thence along the Pastorium property line in an easterly direction, a distance of two hundred twenty-nine (229) feet and seven (7) inches, to the Bradford Street Curb-Stone, a distance of one hundred twenty-two (122) feet and four (4) inches to High Street; thence along High Street at a point where the curb-stone would ordinarily be located, a distance of two hundred twenty-nine (229) feet, more or less, to the beginning corner; being known as the new Central Baptist Church property and being the lot upon which the the New Central Baptist Church has been erected

W. A Keel moderator
Charles E Eidson C. Clerk

56

The Oldest Worship Program

"BRING YE THE WHOLE TITHE NOW"

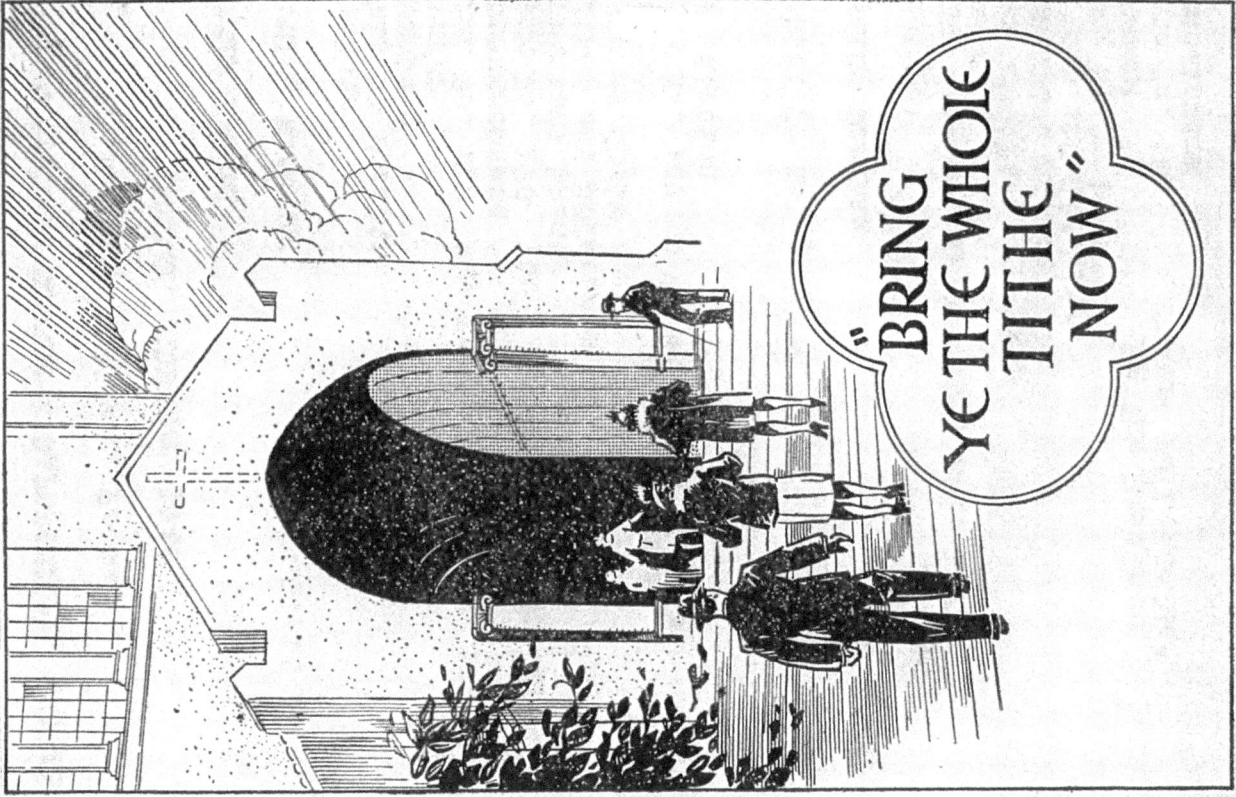

IF WE WANT HIS BLESSINGS WE OUGHT TO ACCEPT HIS PLAN

"BRING YE ALL THE TITHES INTO THE STOREHOUSE AND I WILL POUR YOU OUT A BLESSING MAL 3:10"

TITHES and OFFERINGS
FALSE PROMISES
AMUSEMENTS
TIPS

There are five steps on which folks stop in their financial relation to God. They are:

The Tip Step—They give God a dime as they do the girl that checks their hat. They may even give a quarter, and equal their gratuity to the porter or waiter at their club. Surely God is not pleased by such ungratefulness for His blessings.

The Amusement Step—These folks give when, or if, they attend church. It is on the same level as their patronage of the theatre or baseball park. Others may support the church fifty-two weeks a year. They pay only when they go, or as a government official once put on his pledge card, "$5. per week, when I come". Can we hope for God's blessing on such giving?

The Promise Step—It is a well known fact that many pledge that which they never even try to pay. They impress the church Canvassers with their false "generosity", and do not hesitate to let others know how much "we pledge". What God thinks of this is found in the story of Ananias and Sapphira who made a pledge, had the money to pay it, and then held out on God. They were accused of lying to the Holy Spirit, and their punishment was death. False promises do not merit His blessing.

The Tithe Step—Some believe the law of the tithe to be God's plan for all time and therefore binding on Christians. Honesty requires them to pay it. Others accept it as a fair and reasonable plan for recognizing His ownership and their stewardship. But whether we consider it an obligation or a privilege, surely we ought not to do less as Christians than was required by the law. At any rate, God's challenge has never been recalled, "prove me . . . and see if I will not pour out a blessing".

The Tithe and Offerings Step—The tithe of old was the measure of honesty, but the offerings the evidence of love. God, speaking through Malachi, said, "Ye have robbed me in tithes *and offerings*." The tithe places rich and poor on the same plane. The offerings above the tithe enables the one of large means to show his true appreciation of his greater blessings. May it not be that God is saying to you today as was said to one of old who was occupying a lower place than he should have been, "*Friend, go up higher*".

Layman Tithing Foundation, 8 S. Dearborn St., Chicago 3, Ill.
Printed in the U.S.A.
New Series No. 40

57

CENTRAL BAPTIST CHURCH – GAINESVILLE, GEORGIA

Raymond C. Moore, Pastor

SUNDAY, JUNE 10, 1945

Sunday School   10:00 A. M.

Morning Worship   11:15 A. M.

Prelude
Call To Worship
Doxology
Prayer
Hymn No. 209 "My Faith Looks Up To Thee"
Announcements
Hymn No. 176 "Am I A Soldier Of The Cross"
Scripture Lesson
Tithes and Offerings
Song By Choir
Sermon: By The Pastor
Hymn No. 197 "Only Trust Him"
Benediction

Baptist Training Union   7:00 P. M.

Evening Worship   8:00 P. M.

Prelude
Song Service, Hymns, 185, 130, 167
Prayer
Announcements
Scripture Lesson
Tithes and Offerings
Song By Choir
Sermon: By The Pastor
Hymn No. 164 "Where He Leads Me"
Benediction

58

PASTOR'S COLUMN

Our Daily Vacation Bible School which concluded this Wednesday has been most successful. With an enrollment of 185 and an average attendance of 165 it has set a record. The faculty of 25 capable teachers is especially to be commended for the excellent cooperation which has marked the work from the first day. Each teacher has worked faithfully to make the school what it is – a place where boys and girls follow a Bible–centered program of study, music, handcraft and recreation in an atmosphere of genuine Christian love.

We invite you – especially every parent – to be with us for Commencement this Wednesday evening at 8:00. An interesting demonstration of what has been learned will be presented and awards will be given to the students.

SERVICE MEN'S PRAYER LIST

Sun. William M. Allison, S 2/C
Mon. Pfc. Wayne H. Alexander
Tue. Sgt. Cleveland Bonnette
Wed. Guy Russell Boleman, A. M. M. 2/C
Thurs. Pfc. James E. Addington
Fri. Pfc. James Blackwell
Sat. J. Carroll Blanchard, Cox.

CALENDAR FOR WEEK

Tue. 7:00 R. A.'s
      7:30 "Dollie Hiett" B.W.C.
Wed. 8:00 Vacation Bible School Commencement. Everyone invited.
Thurs 7:30 Intermediate G. A.'s.

J. E. Owen, Chorister, from 1913, to April 6, 1936, was killed in the 1936 tornado in the Pruitt-Barrett Hardware Company.

From the church minutes: W. H. Smith was elected to serve as Choirster October I, 1947, but his tenure was short because on December 31, 1947, he was elected to serve as acting pastor. He served about 3 months.

STAFF

John Cullen Otwell
FIRST MUSIC DIRECTOR
J. C. Otwell
1896

JOHN EGBERT OWEN
Church Chorister, J. E. Owen
September 13, 1913, to April 6, 1936

Church Chorister, Marvin E. Lawson. He was always willing to help when needed. First, on the scene in October of 1935. He served as assistant to Frank DeLong September 2, 1936. On January 13, 1937, he was elected as Chorister. In 1949, Marvin Lawson and Frank DeLong served as Choir Directors. He served as Interim Music Director from September 4, 1952 until Homer Walker arrived in 1953. Until he went to be with the Lord on January 4, 1975, he served his church.

January 13, 1937
January 5 1949, Choir Director
September 4,1952, Served as Music Director until Homer Walker arrived in 1953.

Frank W. DeLong, Chorister
September 2, 1936
August 4, 1937
September 2, 1942
In 1949, he served as Assistant Choir Director and Marvin E. Lawson served as Choir Director until Rev. Ken Sliger was called in 1950.

The Chorister position changed often. Many years the clerk mentioned that officers had been elected, but failed to list them. Many hours have been devoted to getting the names and dates as correct as possible.

A chorister was a singer and/or choir leader until the term choir member and choir director became a more popular reference point.

M. P. Jones, Chorister
September 8, 1943
October 2, 1946

59

Dr. Scott Patterson
Interim Pastor
July 26, 1956, to October 21, 1956
Again, from October 1959, to January 21, 1960

STAFF

Rev. Kenneth Sliger
Minister of Music and Education
June 15, 1950 to October 1952

Clarence Cox
Minister of Music and Education
October 11, 1951 to October 1952

Homer Henry Walker
Minister of Music and Education
1953, 1954, 1955, to April 1, 1956

Rev. Bob Thompson
Interim Music
When Dr. Scott Paterson was Interim Pastor
in 1956 and again in 1959.

John Henry Dalton
First Minister of Youth
July 1, 1957, to December 1960

Rev. Walter Blackwell
Interim Pastor
April 5, 1961, to August 1961

STAFF

Verne Taylor
Minister of Music and Youth
January 15, 1961, to July 21, 1963

Dr Kenneth Baumgardner
Interim Music
August 1963, to March 1964

Eugene Griffith
Minister of Music and Youth
June 1, 1964, to November 8, 1967

Ernest P. Mason (Ernie) Mason
Music Interim
November 15, 1967, to May 26, 1968

Rev. R. W. Prevost
Interim Pastor
June 9, 1968, to October 1, 1968

Dr. Kenneth Baumgardner
Music Interim
June 5, 1968, 1969, to March 29, 1970

STAFF

W. A. "Bud" Stengell, Jr.
Minister of Music and Youth
March 16, 1970, to August 3, 1976

Marvin Goodman
Minister of Education
July 1, 1972, to June 10, 1973

MINISTER OF MUSIC
George Collins
August 7, 1977-February 11, 1979

INTERIM PASTOR
Dr. J. T. Ford
January 1979-August 1979

MINISTER OF MUSIC
Don Davis
April 12, 1979-July 1980

DON ELROD

Interim Music and Youth
May 25, 1980, to June 29, 1980
Associate Pastor of Outreach and
Administrative Assistant 1980, 1981,
1982, and Associate Pastor from
1983, to February 12, 1984.

62

STAFF

MINISTER OF EDUCATION/YOUTH
David McLendon
July 1980-December 1983

INTERIM MUSIC
C. V. Smith
February 1984-March 1985
MINISTER OF MUSIC
March 1985-February 1994

MINISTER OF EDUCATION/YOUTH
Larry Wilbur
March 17, 1985-December 28, 1986

HISPANIC PASTOR- INTERIM January 27, 1985
Richard R. Richey
FULL-TIME August 1, 1987

MINISTER OF EDUCATION/YOUTH
Richard McWhite
May 1, 1987-January 4, 1991

INTERIM YOUTH DIRECTOR
Danny Newbern
January 1991-May 1992

63

STAFF

SUMMER YOUTH MINISTER
Matt Benson
June to August 1992

MINISTER OF EDUCATION/YOUTH
Dwight Oakes
September 1992-August 1998

INTERIM SPEAKER
Ron Barker
April 1993-February 1994

INTERIM PASTOR
J. B. Graham
March-October 1994

INTERIM MINISTER OF MUSIC
James B. Worley
January-July 1996

64

MINISTER OF MUSIC
Ellis Martin
August 1996-November 2005

STAFF

INTERIM PASTOR
Dr. John Lee Taylor
October 2001-June 2002

MINISTER OF YOUTH
Robby Kerr
September 1998-August 2001

INTERIM ASSOCATE PASTOR
Kevin Ingram
November 2001-November 2002

MINISTER OF YOUTH
Jason Harrison
September 12, 2003-May 2004

ERIC WOODS

65

MINISTER OF YOUTH/MUSIC
Eric Woods
January 29, 2006-November 2006

MINISTER OF YOUTH/MUSIC/OUTREACH
Eddie Simmons
January 28, 2007-April 2018 (Music-Outreach)

OUR NEWEST---SAMUEL H. DOYLE .
Student Youth Minister
September, 2023

STAFF

DIRECTOR OF YOUTH
Bradley Woodruff
2011- December 29, 2013

MINISTER OF YOUTH
Craig Broome
January 5, 2014- December 14, 2017

INTERIM MINISTER OF MUSIC

Jim Gittens
2018 to 2020

INTERIM PASTOR

Rev. Terry Rice
April 2018-March 2019

INTERIM MUSIC MINISTER
Don Elrod
2020

66

Boone Strickland
Assistant Pastor
August 9, 2020

Alice Adams
Childrens Ministry
July 2021

MUSICIANS

MUSIC MINISTRY
Miss Madge Doss (Listed in 1937)
And
Mrs. L. E. Roper
1930's

PIANIST
Florence Payne Hefner
1928 -1945

PIANIST-ORGANIST
Minnie Ola Tatum "Dodie" Franklin
1935-1995

PIANIST
Sue Hunt Tyner
1968

ORGANIST
John G. Hulsey
1993

Colene Martin served as pianist in the 1960's and resigned in the Spring of 1968. She also played for the Adult S. S. Class.

67

TORNADO JUNE 3, 1903

Two tornadoes have devasted portions of our city. One on June 3, 1903, and another on April 6, 1936. The 1903 tornado completely destroyed our first church. It also killed many children who were working on the top floors of the Gainesville Mill Factory. The upper floors collapsed and burned during the storm. Many mothers came looking for their children in the debris and found the worst had happened.

FROM THE 7TH EXTRA OF
THE ATLANTA CONSTITUTION
Plucky City Now Engaged in
  Bringing Dead and injured
  Out of Debris—Relief Train
  From Atlanta Arrives On the
  Scene.
(FIRST DISPATCH TO THE JOURNAL)
FROM A STAFF CORRESPONDENT,
 (THE FIRST TO REACH THE CYCLONE
STRICKEN CITY.)
  "Gainesville, June 1, 9 P. M.–
CYCLONE WHICH STRUCK GAINESVILLE
AT 1:30 THIS AFTERNOON COMPLETELY
DESTROYED THE TOP THREE STORIES OF
THE GAINESVILLE COTTON MILL. AT 8
O'CLOCK THIS EVENING 33 BODIES HAD
BEEN RECOVERED AT THIS POINT."

The Atlanta Journal — SPECIAL EXTRA

TORNADO RAVAGES GAINESVILLE; FIRES BREAK OUT; MANY DEAD

April 6, 1936

THE ATLANTA CONSTITUTION

145 ARE KNOWN DEAD AT GAINESVILLE; UNCONTROLLED FIRES RAVAGING CITY

April 7, 1936

DEATHS IN TUPELO PLACED AT 200, THOUSAND INJURED

Devastation Beyond Belief Found by Rescuers in City That Yesterday Was Beautiful Gainesville

TWIN TORNADOES SHATTER SECTION IN HEART OF TOWN

6-E The Daily Times, Gainesville, Ga., Sun., March 23, 1969

Gainesville's tornado called a triplet

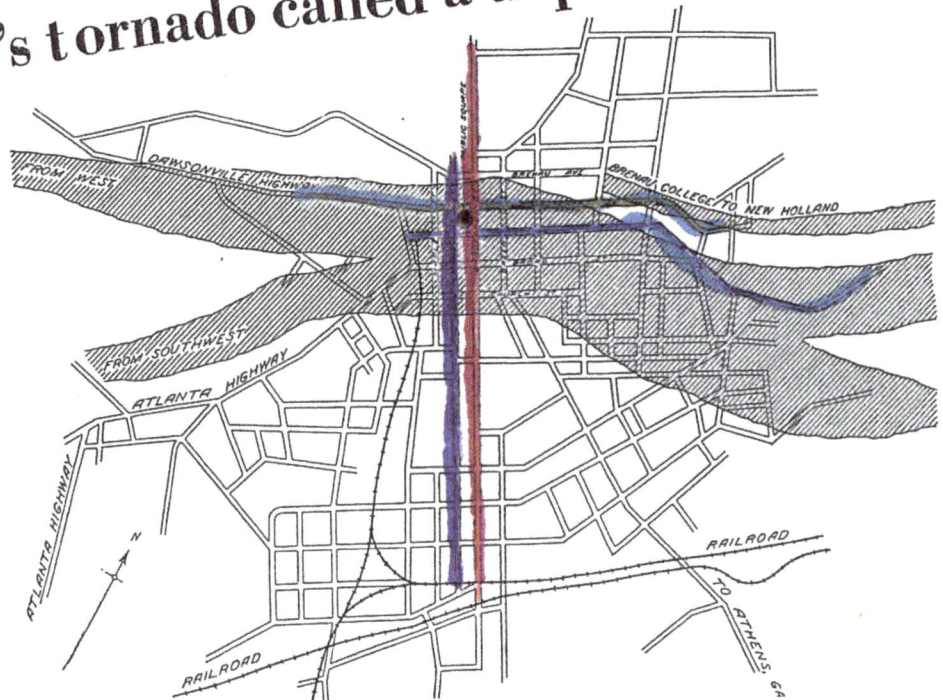

● MAIN STREET

● BRADFORD STREET

● WASHINGTON STREET

● SPRING STREET

● THE SQUARE

CENTRAL BAPTIST CHURCH

"THIS UNUSUAL CHART BY THE UNITED STATES WEATHER BUREAU SHOWS HOW THE THREE-PRONGED TORNADO (OR TORNADOES) SWEPT INTO GAINESVILLE APRIL 6, 1936. AT THE TOP (RIGHT) IS THE PATH OF THE FIRST TWISTER, A SMALL ONE, WHICH STRUCK BRENAU COLLEGE AT 8:27 A.M. AND THEN MOVED ON TOWARD NEW HOLLAND. THE WIDE, CENTER AREA, SHOWS HOW ONE STORM MOVED FROM THE NORTHWEST ALONG THE DAWSONVILLE HIGHWAY. THE OTHER ONE APPROACHED GAINESVILLE FROM THE SOUTHWEST, ALONG THE ATLANTA HIGHWAY. THE TWO FUNNELS CAME TOGETHER WEST OF GROVE STREET, CONVERGED ON THE BUSINESS SECTION AT 8:37 WITH COMBINED FURY AND THEN SEPARATED AND MOVED OUT ALONG DIFFERENT PATHS, PRESUMABLY INTO SOUTH CAROLINA. MOST OLD NEWSPAPER ACCOUNTS REFER TO THE TORNADO AS TWO STORMS, WHEREAS THIS WEATHER BUREAU MAP INDICATES THERE ACTUALLY WERE THREE." (MAP BY COURTESY OF CURTIS VINCENT OF THE GAINESVILLE WESTERN UNION OFFICE.)

TORNADO OF 1936

There was no public warning of the coming of the fury that hit Gainesville on April 6, 1936. The hint on April 5, 1936, 216 people died in Tupelo, Mississippi in a tornado generated by the same front that created the tornado in Gainesville the next day.

Dr. Hartwell Joiner wrote: "I know exactly what time the tornado struck. I saw the watch on the arm of a young boy who had died. The time froze at 8:28 in the morning."

Hartwell Joiner

One of Gainesville's greatest disasters happened on Monday, April 6, 1936. Fourteen city blocks were destroyed when a tornado swept through the city. More than 750 homes were demolished; 250 more were damaged, and the heart of the business area was torn to pieces. Property damage was estimated at more than thirteen million dollars, six million in the business section and seven million in the residential area.

Many people were killed and injured. Approximately 227 people were killed and 750 were seriously injured. People from Atlanta and other places came to help the residents of Gainesville.

There were so many eyewitness stories of tragedies and miracles during and following the tornado of April 6, 1936. The Lord's table located in the Goldie Davis Memorial History Facility was used as a surgeon's table after the tornado. The church served as a rescue mission to the injured and also as a resting place for those who died. The pews of our dear church were filled with the inured and dying.

FROM THE MINUTES OF OUR CHURCH
In the old minute book there is a brief record that reads....
"No conference in April on account of the tornado..."
Of course, history now records that day in April as one of the
dark days in Gainesville Georgia's history when the city was
actually laid waste, almost as if it had been bomed leaving
hundreds of victims.

April 9, 1936
President Franklin D. Roosevelt stopped in Gainesville half an hour Thursday Night following the tornado to speak with the leaders and people of the city who met the train. He expressed his sympathy to everyone in the city and told them the Federal Government is doing everything to make things better for you.

70

THE DAY WE DID NOT HAVE SCHOOL

It was humid and dark that morning when we got on the school bus. The clouds hung long and were black. We lived about ¾ of a mile from the Chestatee River. It was 3 miles from the school. By the time, we got to school it was black outside. We could see a funnel swing down the Dawsonville Highway and drop down about the location of the Chattahoochee River or that was about the distance we thought it must be since we were about 7 miles from Gainesville. A short time later, someone came from Gainesville and told us the storm went across the Chattachooche River and up the valley and hit Gainesville. They told us that Gainesville had been destroyed and there was lots of damage and many people had been killed.

Some children learned their fathers had been killed. Four men had gone to Gainesville that morning and when the tornado hit, they took cover and were killed. They were Mr. Jesse Eades, Mr. Talmadge Stephens, Mr. Murphy , and another man I can not remember.

When we went outside, we saw smoke in the direction of Gainesville. The bus driver carried some of the older boys, several of my brothers were included, to Gainesville the see if they could help in any way.

71

Madge is the mother of Helen M. Martin.

Madge Martin

THE STORM'S TERRIBLE FURY

Randolph Waters and Edward Mays were on their way to the Gainesville High School on the morning of April 6, 1936. Randolph was in the ninth grade. They were walking up Broad and Grove Street and came to St Paul Church. They noticed that it had gotten very dark. It started to rain very hard. They tried to take shelter in the church, but the doors were closed. Randolph said that this was very strange because the doors of the Church had always been open when he passed by going to school.

A man from the Gainesville Midland Railroad Depot called out to them and told them to come inside because a storm was coming. Randolph and Edward went inside and found a hiding place. Randolph said about five minutes later it was light outside. He said that the boxcars had been picked up and dumped on Grove Street. It was a sight to see.

He did not go downtown, but left and started walking.

65th
Anniversary
The
Great Tornado

April 1936-2001
Central
Baptist Church
Gainesville, Georgia

Randolph Waters and his family attended this special tornado remembrance event.

When he came to himself, he was walking home to Armour

Street about ¾ mile away, and still had his books in his hands.

BY THE GRACE OF GOD

St. Paul Church on Grove Street was lifted into the air

where it seemed to hang suspended for a moment. Then it

exploded like a stick of dynamite and disappeared. Its contents-

including heavy pews, an organ, three pianos were never found.

So, as you see, by the grace of God, Randolph Waters and

Edward Mays were saved from the tornado because the church

doors were closed on that particular morning. Every time

Randolph Waters goes by the place, he remembers the very

special corner where he took shelter that morning. It is indeed

a special place. It was a close call , and Randolph was thankful

daily for God's generosity.

Mr. Randolph Waters was a long-time
member of Central. He served as Mayor of
Gainesville, and was a faithful member of the
church. He and his wife, Betty, lived in the
Gainesville area.

RANDOLPH and BETTY WATERS

GRIGG FAMILY VICTIMS OF THE 1936 TORNADO

This information was provided by Ida Jo Grigg McKinney from Waverly, Ohio. She visited our church several years ago and shared this information.

DR. ROBERT DINWIDDIE GRIGG

MR. AND MRS. FRED L. GRIGG

Left to right: CECIL CHESTER, DINWIDDY, NORA ANN AND MALUM GRIGG

I am writing on behalf of the Fredrick LePage Grigg family that lost the most members of one family during the 1936 tornado in Gainesville, Georgia.

Fredrick left his father Robert Dinwiddie at his pharmacy in town and went home to pick up his youngest school age children, Malum age 17, Dinny age 18, Carl Chester age 15, and Clara Margaret age 11, to take to school.

The tornado happened to drop down first that morning on West Avenue where their home was located.

My mother, their oldest child, had already left home for work at Newmans. That building was located in the square downtown and was badly damaged, but my mother lived. She was 21 years old. Her brother, age 19, had already left for school and survived. He was the first one home to find all the rest of the family except for Clara Margaret dead. She was found the next day across the street badly injured. It took her a long time to recover.

Unfortunately Robert Dinwiddie Grigg also died making the total number of seven in that family that died that day. The children's mother and youngest sister Nora age 4, were among that number. They are all buried in Alta Vista Cemetery.

74

IN HONOR AND MEMORY

JOHN EGBERT OWEN

1876– 1936

John Egbert Owen was born July 3, 1876. He was the chorister at Central Baptist Church from 1913 until his death at 8:40 A. M. on April 6, 1936. He was a bookkeeper at the Pruitt-Barrett Hardware Company. The hardware company looked as if it had been bombed and burst into flames when the fifth rated tornado struck Gainesville in 1936.

John also taught the Men's Bible Class, and has a window located in the sanctuary in his honor and memory given by his class. John Egbert Owen was laid to rest at Alta Vista Cemetery on April 16, 1936. He has the distinction of being the longest serving director of music at Central Baptist Church.

MISSIONS

Missions has always been an important part of Central's mission. The

First Sunbeam Band was organized on April 28, 1907. We have had a large

number of boys and girls participate in our mission programs. From 1978,

it has been my honor to work with Mission Friends, Royal Ambassadors,

Girls in Action and Acteens.

Our mission includes a youth trip to Seiling, Oklahoma, working

in a VBS with the Cheyenne Indians. Then, trips to St Petersburg, Florida,

Dauphin Island, Alabama, Jamacia, Montserrat, and local Backyard Bible Clubs.

We currently have an Acteens Program that meets on Wednesday Night. It

is always a joy to dream of a revival of more mission opportunities for our church.

SEILING INDIAN BAPTIST CHURCH
YOUTH VBS --- Seiling, Oklahoma
July 20, 1997

OKLAHOMA CITY AFTER THE BOMBING
Youth Visit ----- July, 1997

I AM A PROMISE
June 14, 1981

Helen Martin, Acteen Director, Luci Cole, Rhonda Cain, Lori Elliott, Shelia Lewis, Kim Mooney, Audrey Smith, Lana Barfield, Shanda Tyner.

Acteens
Queens

Rhonda Cain
Luci Cole
Lori Elliott
Shelia Lewis
Kim Mooney

Queens With A Scepter

Lana Barfield
Audrey Smith
Shanda Tyner

accent

December 1982

Acteens of Central Baptist Church, Gainsville, Georgia, held a recognition service, I Am a Promise.

In the passage from the Bible found in Romans 10:15, Paul says "How beautiful are the feet of them that preach the gospel of peace." This means that the young ladies who have followed the Christian way are individuals described in this passage. From the GAs and Acteens of the past and present we have those who serve as teachers, musicians, nurses, and those who witness by setting the example Christ commanded them to follow.

The Clarion

In Mission Thrust
Let The Church Be Bold

A GREAT HERITAGE
A GREAT FUTURE

Central Baptist Church
"The Church With A Great Sunday Night Service"
Gainesville, Georgia

Truman Collier Skaggs
Pastor
785 Main Street, S.W.
Gainesville, Georgia 30501
404-534-3528

Vol. XVIII   September 18, 1988   No. 32

Helen Martin, Director, Audrey Smith, Shanda Tyner, Kim Moomey, Adina Rooks, Stephanie Dover, Julie Youngs, Susan Davis, Kelly Dover, Lynn Smith, Leader.

FROM THE WMU SCRABOOK 78

Central's June, 1985 ACTEENS Coronation Service published in the January, 1986 Accent Magazine, a publication of the WMU of the Southern Baptist Convention.

CENTRAL BAPTIST CHURCH
June 3, 1984

Audrey Smith

Audrey Smith, we are proud of you! Audrey has earned her Service Aide Citation in the Studiact Individual Achievement Program. This is the final level an Acteen can earn. Audrey is busy in many church activities in addition to her Acteen service. She is a member of the Youth Handbell Choir, the Youth Choir, Sunday School, and participates in surveys and mission trips.

Audrey is a junior at Johnson High School. She is a member of the Beta Club and French Club. She was selected to receive the Georgia Certificate of Merit, an honor extended to students in the top 5 percent of their class. Upon graduation Audrey plans to become a Secondary Education teacher and major in Biological Science. May God keep you in His loving care, Audrey!

Shanda Tyner

Congratulations, Shanda! Shanda Tyner is one of two young ladies who have achieved beyond the four basic levels in the Acteens Studiact Individual Achievement Program. She has earned the Service Aide Citation. In addition to her dedication to the Acteens Organization, Shanda participates in the Youth Choir, Youth Handbell Choir, Sunday School, Church Surveys, Visitation Projects, and has been on several mission trips.

Shanda is an eleventh grader at Johnson High School where she is actively involved in the Band and serves as a Junior Representative in the Octogen Club. Shanda plans to attend college after graduation and major in early elementary education. God bless you, Shanda.

Other Acteens
Sonya Bonner
Marci Summer
Joy Wilbanks

Acteens Director

Helen Martin

G.A. - Acteens Coordinator

Mrs. Susie Martin

It's On My Heart...

By Truman C. Skaggs

Our annual G.A.-Acteen Recognition Service, as you note from this "Clarion," is scheduled for Sunday night at 7:00 o'clock. During all the years I have been pastor at Central this has proven to be one of the truly fine highlights of our mission emphasis throughout the year. This is a rewarding time, not only for our girls and young women who are involved in these mission programs, but it is also rewarding for those who have faithfully led them, and for our entire church. We express our appreciation for the fine leadership of Acteen Director, Helen Martin; G.A. Directors, Polly Mooney, Betty Heathman, Lynne Smith, and Debbie Moody; as well as G.A. and Acteen Coordinator, Mrs. Susie Martin.

Acteens

Queens
Susan Davis
Christi Godfrey
Marie Hunnicutt
Julie Youngs

Queens With A Scepter
Stephanie Dover
Adina Rooks

Queen Regents In Service
Lori Elliott
Kim Mooney

Service Aide Citations
Audrey Smith
Shanda Tyner

THE COMMITMENT CONTINUES
September 18, 1988

Wanda Shores, Christy Godfrey, Melanie Smith, Adina Rooks, Susan Davis, Kelly Dover, Tammy Martin, Melody Smith, Carrie Wood, Jennifer Hulsey.

Lorena Hawkins, Ruby Bell, Cora Lee Quinn, Susie Martin, Clara Howington, Ruby Brown, Grace Boggs, Betty Rooks, Linda Little, Florence Hefner, Lois Hunt.

Central Baptist Church

Gainesville, Georgia

Woman's Missionary Union
Centennial
Acteens Fashion Review

February 12, 1988

Miss WMU 1873 . . . Jennifer Hulsey   Miss WMU 1890 . . . . . Susan Davis   Miss WMU 1900 . . . Melanie Smith

Miss WMU 1910 . . . . Melody Smith   Miss WMU 1920 . . . Tammy Martin   Miss WMU 1926 . . . . . Carrie Wood

Central Baptist Church
Gainesville, Georgia
Woman's Missionary Union
Centennial
Acteens Fashion Review
February 12, 1988

Miss WMU 1930 . .Christy Barfield

Miss WMU 1940 . . . .Wanda Shores

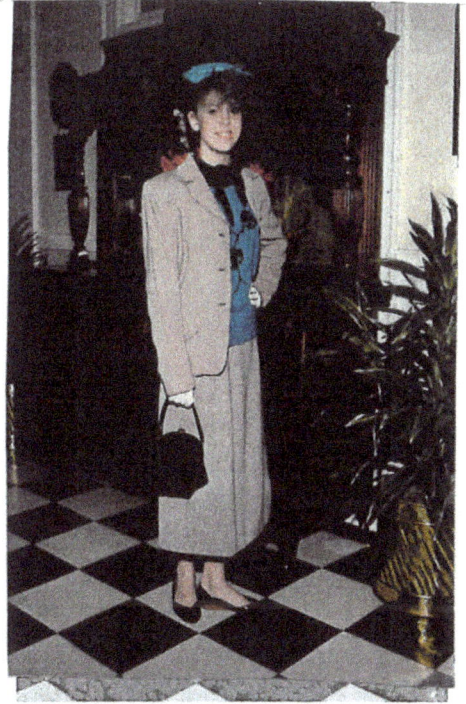

Miss WMU 1950 . . . . . .Kelly Dover

Miss WMU 1960 . .Stephanie Dover

Miss WMU 1970 . . Richenda McWhite

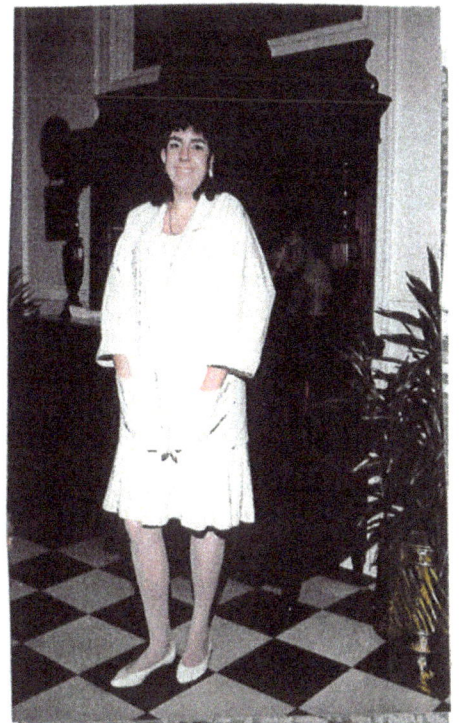

The Future Miss WMU . .Krystee Godfrey

It has been my honor to preside at twenty-two GA Acteens Recognition Services over the last thirty-two years. From 1979 until 1997, the Acteens participated in a program called Studiact. There were Queen-Queen with a Scepter-Queen Regent-Queen Regent in Service,the highest rank in Studiact. Then, the most challenging level of achievement, Service Aide.

At this time, I would like to recognize ladies from the Studiact Program who achieved top levels: Queen Regent In Service—Adina Rooks Cook

Queen Regent In Service—Stephanie Dover

Service Aide—Shanda Tyner Millwood

Service Aide— And Activator -Kelly Dover Hale

Service Aide—Susan Davis Jones

Service Aide— And Activator-Tammy Martin Parsons

MAYSUN AND REBEKAH MARK SPANISH BIBLES FOR VENEZUELA MISSION TEAM

IT'S IN THE BAG. CLARENCE AND WALTER ASSIST THE JAC CLUB #2 MEMBERS IN THEIR PREPARATION OF PACKAGES TO KIDS IN VENEZUELA.

MAYSUN HALE---COMPLETED VENTURES 1-6

FROM THE WMU SCRAPBOOK

Our first recognition service was in 2004 with only G A's. There are six levels in the Missions Ventures Program. We have two young ladies who completed Levels 1-6, Maysun Hale and Mary Elizabthe Pirkle.

THE mag

a Kaleidoscope

June 2010 Vol. 40 #10

HANNAH PIRKLE

Flowery Branch, GA

2010 NATIONAL ACTEENS TOP TEENS

The Acteens Missions program is Called Mission Quest. There are six levels in this latest format. Hannah Prikle is our very first young lady to complete all six levels in Mission Quest. I have had the pleasure of working with Hannah through levels 5, 6 in GAs and all six Mission Quest levels. For those of you who have worked in GAs and Acteens, you know this was no easy task. During the years she worked on Mission Quest, Hannah served as a summer missionary in Venezuela 8 summers with one tour for a two month period of time. The Acteens group earned the Junior American Citizens Community Service Award for the state of Georgia in 2009 and 2010. The highest honor came when Hannah was selected as a National Top Ten Acteen in 2010. Hannah is being honored tonight for completing her last Mission Quest, VISION.

FROM THE WMU SCRAPBOOK

FOLLOWING HIS FOOTSTEPS
May 6, 2012

Kelly Dover Hale, Mayson Hale, Stephanie Dover, Shanda Tyner Millwood, Lauren Chapman, Helen Martin, Acteens Director, Hannah Pirkle, Tammy Martin Parsons, Susan Davis Jones, Mary Elizabeth Pirkle, Connie Johnson, CBA Women's Missionary Team Director.

A GIRLS IN ACTION AND AN ACTEENS REUNION

GIRLS IN ACTION

WORLD VENTURES 4, 5, 6
Lauren Chapman

ACTEENS

MISSIONS QUEST "VISION"
Hannah Pirkle

FROM THE WMU SCRAPBOOK

85

ACTEENS

GIRLS IN ACTION

RECOGNITION SERVICE

May 6, 2012

GAINESVILLE, GEORGIA

ORDER OF SERVICE

Shanda Tyner Millwood

PROCESSIONAL...John Hulsey
                                                            Sue Tyner

BIBLE READING……………………..Susan Davis Jones

WELCOME AND
THEME INTRODUCTION...Helen Martin
CBA Women's Missionary Team Coordinator,   Connie Johnson

SPECIAL MUSIC...............................Shanda Tyner Millwood

RECOGNITION OF SPECIAL GUESTS……….....Helen Martin

PRESENTATION OF AWARDS...................................Helen Martin

MISSION CALENDAR AND PRAYER...Tammy Martin Parsons

SPECIAL MUSIC...............................Shanda Tyner Millwood

CLOSING REMARKS...Hannah Pirkle
                                                            Pastor Earl Pirkle

RECESSIONAL..John Hulsey
                                                            Sue Tyner

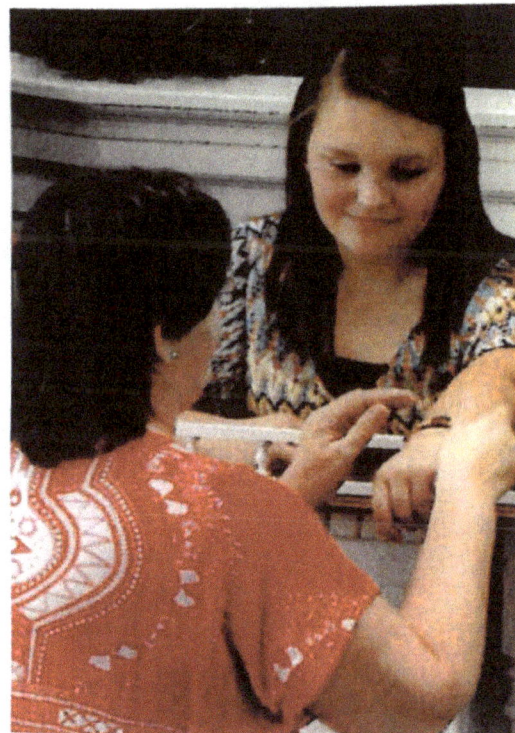

Tonight, it is my very distinct honor to recognize Lauren Chapman. Lauren has completed Mission

Ventures-Levels 4, 5, 6. You will be able to observe some of the work Lauren has completed after

tonight's service.   Lauren, I am proud of you and challenge you to follow the footsteps of Christ as you

mature in your Christian faith. Please accept your charm bracelet and charms.

SYDNEY PARSONS

RECOGNITION CEREMONY

JORDYN   DAD, PHILLIP   SYDNEY

JORDYN PARSONS

ESTHER   AND   MARTHA

Mama Tammy

SYDNEY   PASTOR MIKE   JORDYN

Today's Acteen

A challenge from your Acteen Leader: "I challenge you to be an example to others as you demonstrate a life of faith in a changing and challenging world. I challenge you to love and accept those in need of Christ in their life. I further challenge you to witness and represent Christ in a lost world. Lastly, I challenge you to represent our King well, to let His light shine through you."

Love and blesings,   Ms Helen

87

SANCTUARY CHOIR

ROW 1 Truman C. Skaggs, Wanda Bonds, Debbie Moody, Dell Moody, C. V. Smith, Jo Mare McLendon, Lynn Smith, Sue Tyner, Terry Matthews, Murphy Lanning.

ROW 2 Don Elrod, Dodie Franklin, Evelyn Baker, Jimmy Bagwell, Mark Winchester, Betty Rooks, Louise Tolbert, Helen Martin, David McLendon.

Row 3 Buck Cochran, Walter Waldon, Wayne Parrish, Alan Sutton, John Hunnicutt, Hal Chitwood, Jack Pethel, Anna Prince.

Life is a song, Love is the music.

ROW 1 Phyllis Simmons, Jan Cobb, Myrtle Smith, Betty Rooks, Doris Watson, Judy Arrowsmith, Pat Carroll, Kathy Perry, Helen Martin.

ROW 2 Diane Connell, Kay Smith, Hannah Pirkle, Mary Elizabeth Pirkle, Jennifer Trawick, Michelle Eubanks, Lauren Chapman, Sherry Pirkle, Colene Martin.

ROW 3 Betty Heathman, Josh Cofield, Thor Smith, Tony Walker, Walter Smith, Jim DeLay, David Eubanks, David Smith, Bradley Woodruff, Earl Pirkle.

Director: Mr. Eddie Simmons

SPORTS FUN AND RECREATION

1951 Winning Team

ROW 1   Gerald Gailey,   Williams, Verla Smith, Robert Sims, Walter Smith, Paul Sims
ROW 2   Jack Hudgins, Terry Brown, David Martin
ROW 3   Gordon People, Jimmy Lewis, James Pethel, Curtis Pethel, Jimmy Grindle

90

CENTRAL BAPTIST CHURCH SOFTBALL TEAM

1968

Front Row - Left to Right

Tom Hall
Randall Smallwood
Jim Gittens
Burl Maddox
Bill Carey
Ron McClure
Bob Watson

Back Row-Left to Right

Doug Bonds
Benny Pethel
Don Waldrip
Clarence Bales
Frankie Allison
Loy Bonds

Local sports became a fun activity and an integral part of social life in the 1950's and 60's. It became a fun place to go, and a place for Christian fellowship and a good time for gathering together.

GAINESVILLE

1909
Busy Day In Gainesville, Ga.

ESTES BUTLERS

GAINESVILLE–A CHANGING CITY

The Cherokee Indians gave up their land where we live on July 8, 1817. Then, the land was divided into counties. On December 5, 1818, Hall County was formed. Hall County was named in honor of Dr. Lyman Hall one of the signers of the Declaration of Independence. Governor John Clark, Governor of Georgia, approved a charter for Gainesville to start a city on April 21, 1821. Justice John Vance Cotter, one of five justices, suggested the name of General Edmund Pendleton Gaines. General Gaines was a hero in the War of 1812, and the city was named after him. The land was surveyed by Timothy Terrell IV, a civil engineer, with seventy-four lots. One lot was reserved for a public square, a court house and two churches.

Gaineville grew slowly. It is hilly and hard to farm. Gold was discovered in North Georga in 1928. Gainesville became the trading center for gold miners. In 1829, there were thirty-one homes and fifteen businesses. Many people moved here because of the gold rush, and when it ended, they just moved away. Gainesville was almost destroyed by fire in December 1851. Two other fires in 1873 and 1876 did a great deal of damage to the city.

When the railroad came to the city there had to be a way to move lots of cotton to the depot, and a trolley was the answer. Also, lots of people came to enjoy the warm springs that were nearby. The trolley ran in Gainesville from 1874 until 1927. The city grew from a population in 1872 to 4,000 in 1888.

Central Baptist Church enters the picture as a mission in 1891.

HISTORICAL MARKING OF CENTRAL

CENTRAL
BAPTIST *CHURCH*
785 Main Street
Gainesville, GA

CELEBRATING
130 YEARS

January 30, 1890

January 26, 2020

~ Matthew 22: 37-40 ~

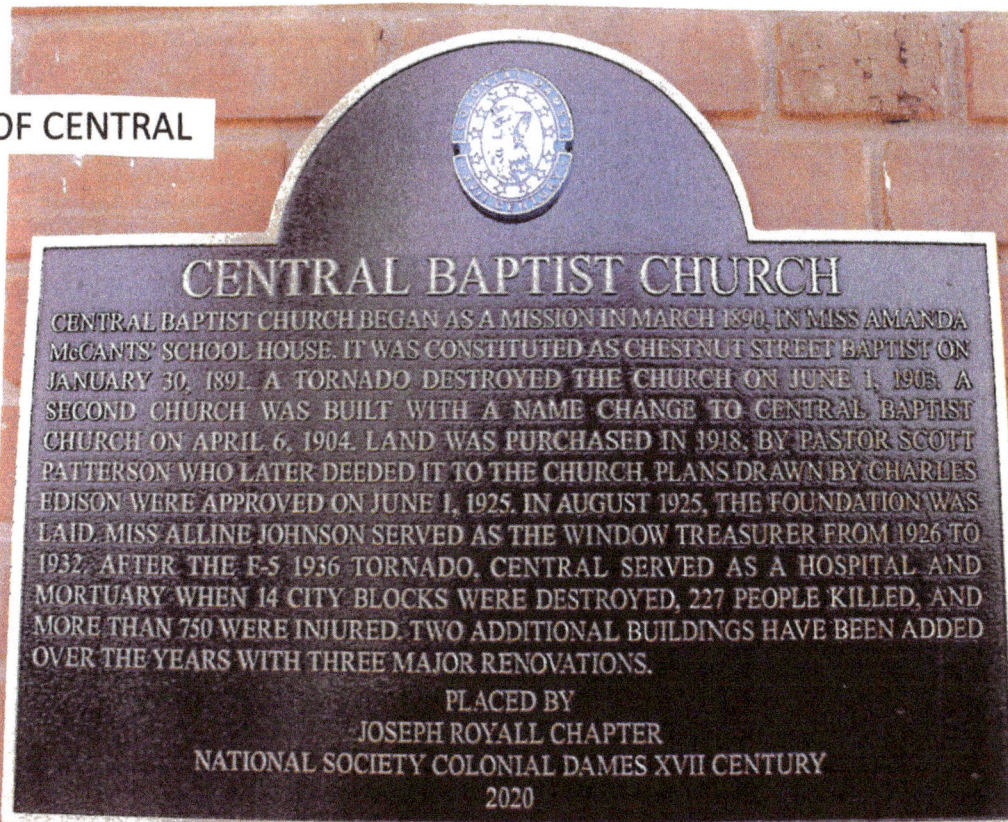

Central Baptist Church
785 Main St. SW
P.O. Box 444
Gainesville, GA 30503
www.centralbaptistgainesville.com

October 16, 2019

Helen Martin
1345 Lakeshore Circle
Gainesville, GA 30501

Dear Helen:

This letter constitutes permission for you to proceed with plans to order and then place a historical marker provided by the National Society Colonial Dames XVII Century, approximately 12" x 18" in size and bronze in composition. The agreed-upon placement of the marker will be on the front size porch of the church building located at 785 Main Street here in Gainesville.

The occasion for placing the marker will be the 130th anniversary of the Central Baptist Church ministry in Gainesville and Hall County, Georgia. A tentative target for placing the marker will be sometime in January, 2020.

Thank you for combining your passions for both history of our community and your dedication to our church family!

Sincerely,

Michael E. Taylor
Pastor, Central Baptist Church

MISS HELEN M. MARTIN HISTORIAN OF THE JOSEPH ROYALL CHAPTER, CDXVIIC, AND HISTORIANOF CENTRAL BAPTIST CHURCH WELCOMES EVERYONE AND SPEAKS TO THE SIGNIFICANCE OF THE HISTORICAL MARKING OF CENTRAL BAPTIST CHURCH, SEPTEMBER 9, 2020.

CENTRAL BAPTIST CHURCH

CENTRAL BAPTIST CHURCH BEGAN AS A MISSION IN MARCH 1890, IN MISS AMANDA McCANTS' SCHOOL HOUSE. IT WAS CONSTITUTED AS CHESTNUT STREET BAPTIST ON JANUARY 30, 1891. A TORNADO DESTROYED THE CHURCH ON JUNE 1, 1903. A SECOND CHURCH WAS BUILT WITH A NAME CHANGE TO CENTRAL BAPTIST CHURCH ON APRIL 6, 1904. LAND WAS PURCHASED IN 1918, BY PASTOR SCOTT PATTERSON WHO LATER DEEDED IT TO THE CHURCH. PLANS DRAWN BY CHARLES EDISON WERE APPROVED ON JUNE 1, 1925. IN AUGUST 1925, THE FOUNDATION WAS LAID. MISS ALLINE JOHNSON SERVED AS THE WINDOW TREASURER FROM 1926 TO 1932. AFTER THE F-5 1936 TORNADO, CENTRAL SERVED AS A HOSPITAL AND MORTUARY WHEN 14 CITY BLOCKS WERE DESTROYED, 227 PEOPLE KILLED, AND MORE THAN 750 WERE INJURED. TWO ADDITIONAL BUILDINGS HAVE BEEN ADDED OVER THE YEARS WITH THREE MAJOR RENOVATIONS.

PLACED BY
JOSEPH ROYALL CHAPTER
NATIONAL SOCIETY COLONIAL DAMES XVII CENTURY
2020

HISTORICAL MARKING–130TH ANNIVESARY

AREA WHERE MARKER WILL BE PLACED

Anniversary 130th Celebration

Marking the 130th Anniversary of

CENTRAL BAPTIST CHURCH

785 Main Street

Gainesville, Georgia 30501

September 9, 2020

11 O'clock am

1890 – 2020

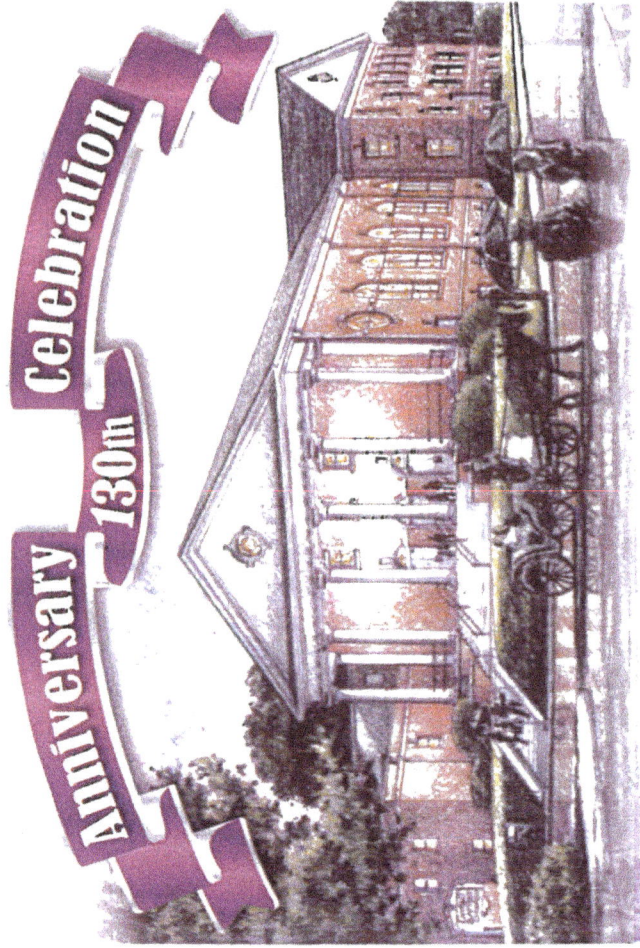

PRESENTED BY:

Joseph Royall Chapter (GA27)
Colonial Dames XVII Century

A SPECIAL NOTE OF THANKS:

Mrs. Patricia Everts, National Chairman of Marking and Preservation of Historic Sites for her leadership and assistance in getting Central Baptist Church approved for this honor.

Mr. Danny Faulkner, Memorial Park, Funeral Home; Installation of the plaque.

Mrs. Marcie Fletcher, Chaplain, Joseph Royall Colonial Dames Chapter, For much moral support and providing the invitations.

Mrs. Dot Floyd, Central Baptist Church; Preparation of invitations for mailing,

Mrs. Sherryll Miles, State President, Colonial Dames of the 17thCentury. Approved a $500 scholarship for use toward purchase of the plaque.

Mr. Bud Savage, Central Baptist Church. Photographs and set-up assistance.

Sound Technicians: Matt Trawick and Mike Motkowski.

Rev. Mike Taylor, and Deacons, Central Baptist Church, for believing that we could move forward with the tribute for our beautiful church.

Other donations were given by:
Mr. Clarence Barnett
Mr. Heyward Hosch
Mr. Harvey Rooks

A GRATEFUL THANK YOU TO ALL MEMBERS OF THE JOSEPH ROYALL CHAPTER. COLONIAL DAMES CDXVIIC.

95

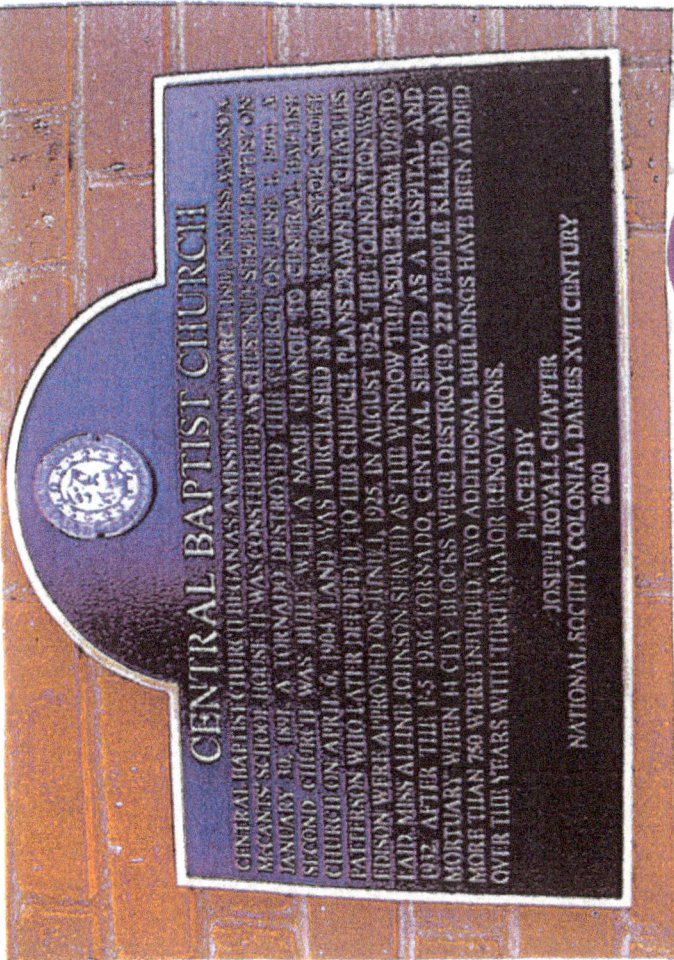

CENTRAL BAPTIST CHURCH

CENTRAL BAPTIST CHURCH BEGAN AS A MISSION IN MARCH 1888. FAMILIES AROUND MCCANTS SCHOOL HOUSE 1 MILE WAS CONSTITUTED AS A CHURCH ON SEPTEMBER 23, 1888. THE JANUARY 12, 1889, A TORNADO DESTROYED THE CHURCH. ON JUNE 15, 1890, A SECOND CHURCH WAS BUILT WITH A NAME CHANGE TO CENTRAL BAPTIST. THE CHURCH ON APRIL 6, 1904, LAND WAS PURCHASED IN 1918, BY PASTOR SCOTT. PATTERSON WHO LATER DEEDED IT TO THE CHURCH. PLANS DRAWN BY CHARLES. HUDSON WERE APPROVED ON JUNE 1, 1925. IN AUGUST 1925, THE FOUNDATION WAS LAID. MISS ALINE JOHNSON SERVED AS THE WINDOW TREASURER FROM 1926 TO 1932. AFTER THE 1-5 BIG TORNADO, CENTRAL SERVED AS A HOSPITAL AND MORTUARY. WITHIN 11 CITY BLOCKS WERE DESTROYED, 227 PEOPLE KILLED, AND MORE THAN 750 WERE INJURED. TWO ADDITIONAL BUILDINGS HAVE BEEN ADDED OVER THE YEARS WITH THREE MAJOR RENOVATIONS.

PLACED BY
JOSEPH ROYALL CHAPTER
NATIONAL SOCIETY COLONIAL DAMES XVII CENTURY
2020

Great is Thy Faithfulness

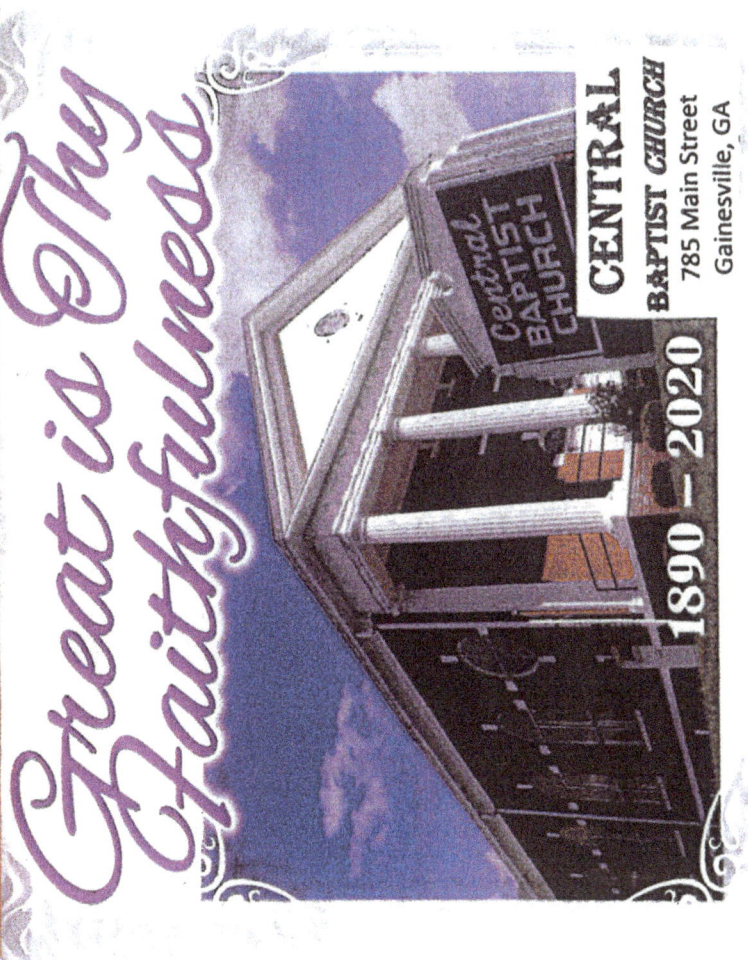

CENTRAL
BAPTIST CHURCH
785 Main Street
Gainesville, GA

1890 – 2020

ORDER OF THE PROGRAM

Invocation..Mr. Jim DeLay, Deacon
Central Baptist Church

Presentation of Flags...............United States Flag..........Colonel Kevin Jarrard
United States Marine Corps

Christian Flag.............Miss Alice Adams
Central Baptist Church

Pledge to the Bible..............Deacon Boone Strickland
Central Baptist Church, Associate Pastor

Colonial Dames 17th Century Flag: Mrs. Sheryll Taylor Miles, State President

Welcome...Miss Helen M. Martin, Historian
Chairman, Marking and Preservation of Historic Sites
Joseph Royall Chapter, Colonial Dames 17th Century

Introduction of Guests..............Mrs. Patricia "Pat" Calmes, President
Joseph Royall Chapter, Colonial Dames 17th Century

Rev. Mike Taylor, Pastor
Central Baptist Church

Mr. Don Elrod

Special Music..."America"
Minister of Music, Central Baptist Church

Introduction of Speaker.............................Rev. Mike Taylor, Pastor
Central Baptist Church

Speaker..Colonel Kevin Jarrard
United States Marine Corps

Dedication of Marker...............................Miss Helen M. Martin, Historian
Marking and Preservation of Historic Sites - Joseph Royall Chapter, CDXVIIC
Participants:
Rev. Mike Taylor, Pastor
Central Baptist Church

Mr. Harvey Rooks, Deacon
Central Baptist Church

Mrs. Sherryll Taylor Miles, State President
Colonial Dames 17th Century

Mrs. Phyllis Hill King, State Chaplain
Colonial Dames 17th Century

Benediction...Colonial Dames 17th Century

THE MARKING OF THE CHURCH TODAY IS PRESENTED BY THE JOSEPH

ROYALL CHAPTER, COLONIAL DAMES CDXVIIC.

Dr. Charles Drake, Rev. Truman C. Skaggs, and Rev. Larry Tomlin.

Floyd Smith, Jack Pethel, and Wilburn Peeples.

Pamela Lockhart

Terry Lockhart

97

GLENN – BRENDA CANADA

Don and Martha Elrod

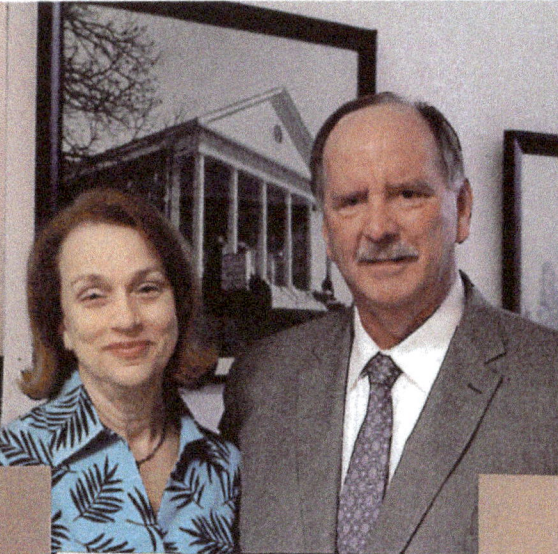

GEORGE HOPE

Jo Marie and David McLendon

ROBERT - PAT CARROLL

Don & Priscilla Davis

Earl and Bea Levine

Walter and Myrtle Smith

DAVID – LINDA DOVER

TOKKIE – DR. CHARLES DRAKE

Sam and Jean Curtis

FRANCES – GEORGE WILEY

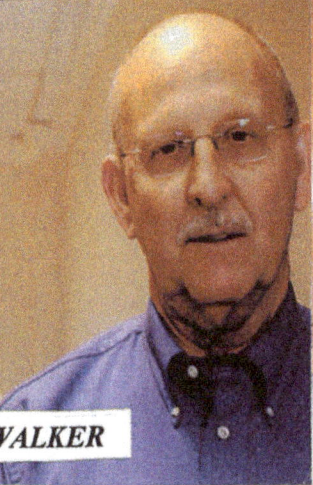

MICKI – TONY WALKER

98

LOUISE TOLBERT

Charlotte and Morris McClure

Pastor Milke and Allison Taylor

Jim and Sue Gittens

Jennifer and Matt Trawick

THANK YOU, GENTLEMEN!!!

SUNDAY SCHOOL WATERMELON CUTTING ----------Dee Bell, Bud Savage, Clarence Barnett, and Walter Smith.

Jan Cobb

Sunday School

SUNDAY SCHOOL ROUND UP-----Ray Matin, Colene Martin, Boone Strickland, Joann Reese, and Ann Strickland.

Joann Reese wears her mother's hat.

Betty Sewell Smith, Doris Watson, Teacher, Henrietta Bennett, Lois Hope, Ruby Massey, Elizabeth Lenderrnan, Louise Tolbert, Doris Rogers, "Little Bit" Hulsey, Rebecca Scroggs, Sarah Henson.   (Sarah Henson, Jane Baker, and Eloise Baxter were sisters.)

ERGATAN SUNDAY SCHOOL cLASS

100(a)

Eloise

Jane

SUE MARTIN

CENTRAL BAPTIST CHURCH   GAINESVILLE, GEORGIA

Ergatan Sunday School Class - June - December 1946.

Teacher   -   E. Toy Owen   SUNDAY SCHOOL REPORT

Ergatan   -   Workers

Motto   -   "What would Jesus Have Me Do?"

Officers:

President   -   Mrs. Kennon J. Ward
Secretary   -   Mrs. H. P. Morrison
Treasurer   -   Mrs. C. R. Howington

Groupe 1

Bernice Nix - Captain
Fay Deaton   - A
Mrs. H. P. Morrison
Mrs. J. R. Mcever
Mrs. J. L. Lawson
Mrs. Grace Price
Sylvia Slaton
Mrs. H. R. Seay
Jennie Smith
Mary Lenderman
Azslee Pittman
Sadie Reed
Bernice Martin
Mrs. Robert Lenderman
Jeanette Smith

Groupe 2

Mrs. Ora Johnson, - Captain
Clara Howington
Annie Mae McKinney
Louise Tolbert
Mrs. John Logan
Mrs. Carl Hynie
Mrs. Cleon Bennett
Bonnie Conner
Utah Simmons
Claudine Stewart
Mrs. M. J. McCoy
Claudia Roper

SUNDAY

SCHOOL

FROM THE SCRAPBOOK OF
MRS. LESSIE MILLER
JUNE – DECEMBER 1946

Groupe 3

Margaret McIntyre, - Captain
Inez Owen
Mrs. Harry Brown
Noami Orr
Mrs. Ellis Lenderman
Ruth Henderson
Mrs. Clark
Louise Eberhardt
Mrs. Gilstrap
Mrs. Odis Kiser
Doris Phillips.

Groupe 4

Lessie Miller - Captain
Mrs. Eugene Hollis
Mrs. W. H. Kesler
Noami Thomas
Mrs. Lee Conner
Mrs. Rad Bonds
Mrs. C. R. Franklin
Beatrice Rogers
Carolyn Cochran
Mrs. James Thompson

Aim   - - - - - - -   Goal
To walk Life's road with shoulders square,   To constantly improve my mind,
To keep my vision true and fair,   To strive through effort hard to
And spread contentment everywhere -   find
     Is my aim   Success, yet keep my spirit kind -
                                                   Is my goal

Creed

To do my best from day to day
To claim a share of work and play,
To live as humbly as I pray -
     Is my creed.
          100(b)   A. H. Barr.

Junior Department:
Superintendent — Mrs. Amos E. Norman
Asso. Supt. - Chor. — C. R. Franklin
Secretary — Amos E. Norman
Pianist — Miss Cammie N. Still
Teachers
Mrs. Winifred Conner - Miss Lillian Moss
Mrs. J. L. Allison - Mrs. T. L. Carlton
Mr. Joe L. Brown - Mr. K. G. Brown
Mrs. V. B. Waldrip - Mr. Horace Luther
Mrs. Whitfield

Intermediate Department:
Superintendent — H. D. Greenway
Asso. Supt. — Mrs. Rafe Luther
Secretary — Mrs. Ruby Greenway
Teachers
Miss Montine Tidwell - Mrs. Alvin Gailey
Mr. L. E. Hatfield - Mr. H.T. Jarrard
Mrs. Cleveland Bonnette - Mrs.R.S.Ramsey
J. M. Lancaster - A. O. Miller

Young People's Department:
Superintendent — Max J. Green
Secretary — Robert Norman, Jr.
Teachers — H. E. Lendermen
Mrs. W. J. Schimmel
Mrs. R. C. Moore

Adult Department:
Superintendent — Mr. J. L. Hulsey
Secretary — T. O. Culpepper
Chorister — M. E. Lawson
Pianist — Mrs. C. R. Franklin
Teachers
J. A. Crumbley - M. P. Jones
Mrs. J.L.Hulsey - Mrs.Reba McDonald
Toy Owen E. H. Still

A SAD NOTE IS THAT SOMETIMES REPORTS ARE MADE AND NOT RECORDED BY THE CLERK AT THE TIME THEY ARE ACCEPTED. THE PAPER REPORTS ARE OFTEN LOST BECAUSE OLD GLUE DISCOLORED OR FAILED TO PROPERLY PASTE DOCUMENTS INTO BOOKS. THE TWO PAGES FROM MRS. LESSIE MILLER'S SCRAPBOOK ARE VERY RARE AND PRICELESS. THESE PAGES WERE GIVEN BY HER SON, FLETCHER MILLER. HER DAUGHTER IS GLENDA MILLER PIERCE.

FROM THE SCRAPBOOK OF
MRS. LESSIE MILLER

SUNDAY SCHOOL OFFICERS AND TEACHERS

October 1946 - 1947

General Officers:
Superintendent — Herbert F. Lewis
Asso. Supt. — S. R. Merritt
Asso. Supt. — Mrs. Raymond C. Moore
Secretary — Miss Willie Taylor

Cradle Roll Department:
Superintendent — Mrs. J. N. Gailey
Asso. Supt. & Sect.— Mrs. R. L. McMahan
Visitor — Mrs. Glenn Tidwell
Workers
Mrs. Joe Brown Mrs. Herbert Lewis
Mrs. Roy Sheridan Miss Elizabeth Gailey
Mrs. Joe Stovall

Beginner Department:
Superintendent — Mrs. T. O. Culpepper
Asso. Supt.-Sect. — Mrs. M. E. Lawson
Pianist — Mrs. Joyce King
Workers
Mrs. Dave Crowe - Mrs. Ed Wall
Mrs. S. R. Merritt - Mrs. C. P. Stewart
Mrs. Broadus Kiser

100(c)

Primary Department:
Superintendent — Mrs. A. E. Prince
Asso. Supt. — Mrs. Clyde Quinn
Pianist — Mrs. J. M. Lancaster
Secretary — Mrs. Max J. Green
Teachers
Miss Dot Leckie - Miss Marion Martin
Miss Christine Hale - Mrs. B. H. Moore
Mrs. Clyde Grindle - Mrs. G. W. Binns
Mrs. Harry Brown

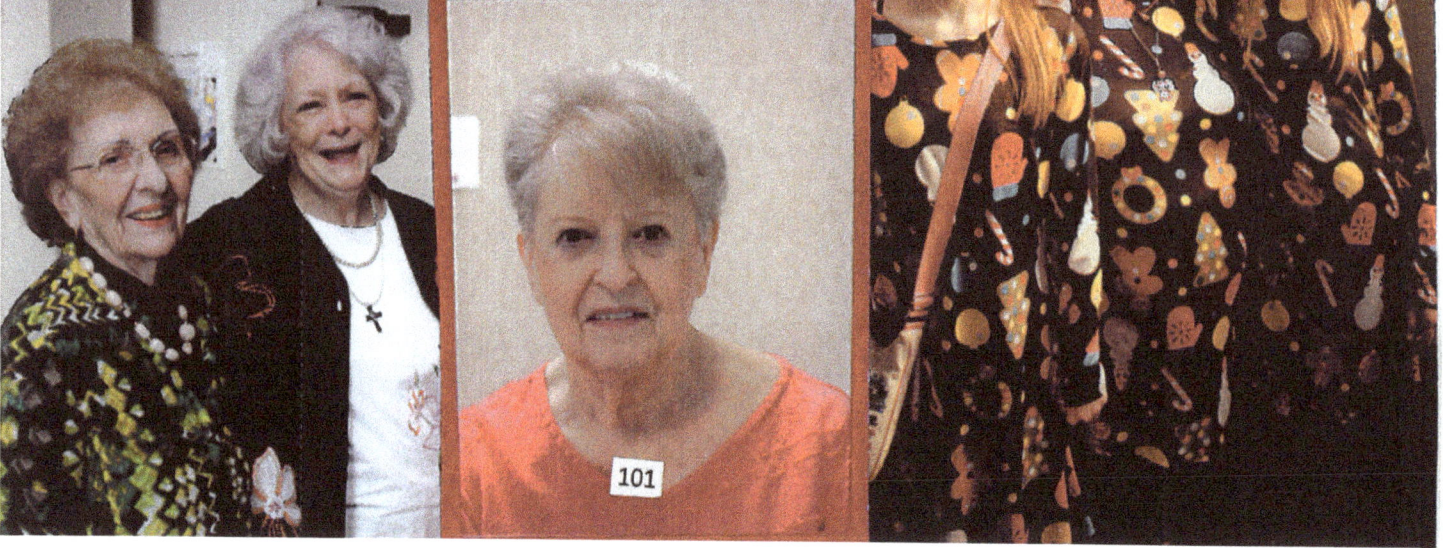

101

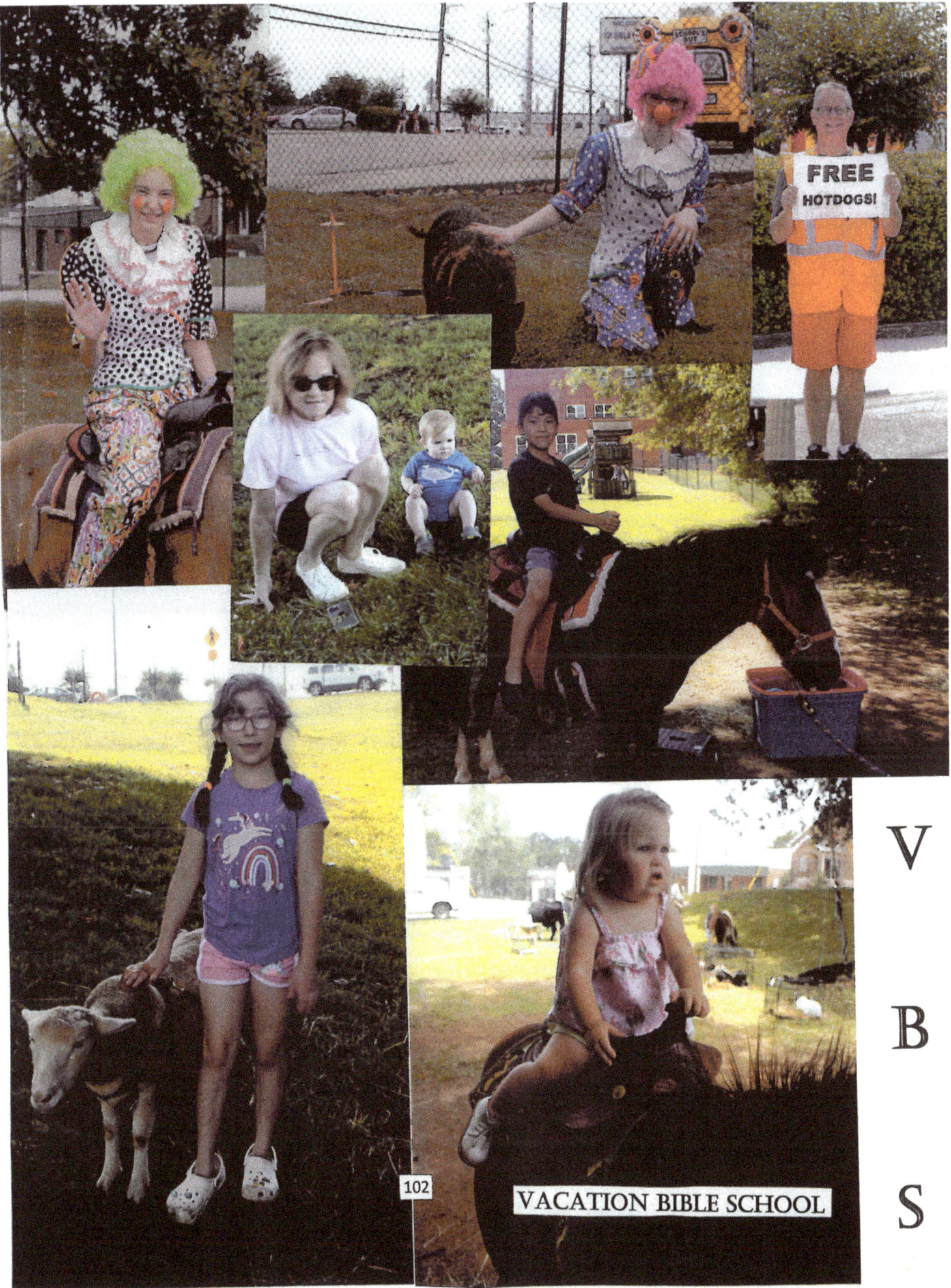

FREE HOTDOGS!

VACATION BIBLE SCHOOL

V
B
S

104

105

107

Central Baptist Church Sunday School - 1959

(Dr. Bates last Sunday)

PALM SUNDAY — APRIL 11, 1976

CENTRAL'S BICENTENNIAL PICTURE

Dr. Charles Stanley, Pastor of the First Baptist Church, Atlanta, Georgia, was guest preacher at the Harvest Revival on October 10-13, 1982, at Central. Truman C. Skaggs was Central's Pastor.

A SALUTE TO OUR VETERANS

Central has always recognized Veterans for their service to our country. In World War II the church purchased war bonds in support of the war effort. The church has a special event on all holidays to give honor for their contributions made to our country. For many years Betty Heathman has spear-headed the "Quilts of Valor" Program for veterans as a special token of love and deep appreciation. Every quilt is handmade. The Girls in Action, the Acteens, and adults have made care packages, cards, etc. to send to our veterans in hospitals, in nursing homes and overseas.

A local group of Korean Veterans had a meeting at Central for a number of years with a special meal prepared for them.

Betty Heathman presents Jim DeLay with a handmade "Quilt of Valor" honoring his Naval Service.

Clarence A. Barnett, Jr. served in the Army.

Book Two
The Windows

CENTRAL BAPTIST CHURCH

CENTRAL BAPTIST CHURCH, NOT AN IMPOSSIBLE DREAM,

BUT A GOD DREAM THAT CAME INTO FRUITION

Bud Savage, Artist

There are ninety-eight stained glass windows adorning our beautiful church. The maker of the windows has not been found or recorded. We have a few facts from old WMU scrapbooks. The baptismal widow was purchased in 1930 by the WMU for $275. The triple windows in the sanctuary were purchased for $122. for each set. There has been no record found for the large round windows and all the others. When the atrium was being constructed, some windows were moved and installed in the new atrium.

H.D. WALLACE AND H.D. TANNER

TABLE OF CONTENTS

CENTRAL BAPTIST CHURCH, NOT AN IMPOSSIBLE DREAM, BUT A GOD DREAM THAT CAME INTO FRUITION

Our beautiful church, Central Baptist Church, was built for God's purpose and with His Grace by hard-working men, women and children. The idea of building a new house of worship was conceived in 1919. Dr. Scott Patterson was elected Pastor on September 4, 1919. The dream to build a new church was not realized because of the shortage of money until Dr. Patterson bought the current church property on Main Street. He deeded the property to Central Baptist Church on February 11, 1920. This transition was recorded in Book 38, page 20, July 16, 1920, at the Hall County Court Clerk's office.

In the spring of 1923, the Woman's Missionary Union started a building fund. They also had a Christmas Bazaar to raise money.

On motion, June 1, 1925, the church voted to build a new church. Also, the plans submitted by Charles Edison were accepted. The Chairman for the Finance Committee for the new church building was J. J. Hudgins. The Moderator, T.W. Selman, appointed E.A. Burchfield, Charles Edison, J. E. Owen and W.H. Stewart as the Building Committee. In addition, on motion, the church voted to conduct a drive on Sunday, June 14, 1925, to raise funds for the new building.

On August 12, 1925, the Building Committee was authorized to purchase materials for laying the foundation for the new church. The church extended a vote of thanks to the city for the work they did on the church lot.

In August 1925, the foundation for the new church was laid. On December 2, 1925, the Church, on motion, instructed the Building Committee to have the exterior of the foundation walls coated with tar. The basement would be used for church services. The last church service was held in the old church on Myrtle and Maple Streets on December 5, 1926. This church had been used for twenty-three years. In March 1926, the Myrtle and Maple Street property was offered for sale for $4,000. It sold on August 12, 1928, to the Salvation Army for $1,000.

In conference, June 2, 1926, the church voted to have a citywide canvas to secure funds to complete the new church building. The date was set for July 18-25, 1926. This was one of the first efforts to reach out to the Gainesville area for financial help.

On March 28, 1926, Horace Fuller resigned as treasurer for the new building fund. Miss Aline Johnson was elected as treasurer for this fund. The building fund and the church treasury fund were handled separately.

The recorded story of the church's stained-glass windows begins at this point. In 1927, the Woman's Missionary Union contributed $122 for three windows in the church. Rev. R. D. Hawkins' name was to be placed on one.

May 16, 1928, Dr. W.A. Keel from Louisville, Kentucky, was unanimously called to be Pastor of our church at a salary of $1,800 with house included. On June 27, 1928, on recommendation of the Building Committee and

2

The Board of Deacons, the church voted to raise $8,000 from its members to resume work on the new church building. On completion of this drive, a canvas of the city for a like amount was to be made. Rev. W. A. Keel was the Moderator, and Charles Edison was Church Clerk.

The first brick was laid on June 9, 1928. Mrs. Ruby Maddox (Barbara Hall's mother) told of the times her father, Mr. J. L. Allison, worked on the church building. She said he was there when the foundation was laid and when the bricks were laid. When she and Mr. Burl Maddox got married, tithing was one thing they started and never stopped. Mrs. Cora Lee Quinn (Becky Herrington's mother) was the daughter of Mr. J. L. Allison. Becky's father was Mr. Hugh Quinn. Margie Webb's father, Mr. William "Buck" Allison, was the son of Mr. J. L. Allison.

On November 7, 1928, the Building Committee was instructed to work out plans to finish the cornice and gables of the new church building.

On February 6, 1929, Miss Alline Johnson tendered her resignation as the Building Fund Treasurer. On motion, this was not accepted, motion prevailed to pay her $10.00 a month if she would continue to serve as Treasurer.

On October 20, 1929, the Trustees, B. H. Moore, W. B. Reed and Charles E. Edison were authorized to sign papers for the loan of $10,000 from the Home Mission Board to complete the building of the church. (This loan was paid off in 1942.) The church voted to register the name, style and object of the church with names of Trustees in Hall County Superior Court.

"SPEAKING OF HARD TIMES," June 4, 1930, the church voted to
employ a collector for the local expenses of the church – said collector to
receive 10% of collections. Keep in mind the church was still in a building
program, still owed money borrowed from the Home Mission Board and
had regular church expenses. What a debt we owe the brave members
of our church during the depression days!

This appeared in The Gainesville Eagle, December 4, 1930.

NEW WINDOW AT CENTRAL CHURCH

"An ornamental window of stained glass to be placed above the baptistery in
the church will be bought by the WMU of Central, according to plans made at
the last business meeting. This window will cost $275. It is hoped it will be
in place by the end of the month."

According to a story related to me years ago, Mrs. E.A. Burchfield embroidered
on a quilt the name of everyone who gave a dime for the purchase of this
window. What a gift she gave to the church. God blessed her for this effort.

On June 3, 1931, all funds were consolidated, regular and building, except the
Home Mission Board payments. Miss Alline Johnson, who had tried to resign
earlier from the awesome job of keeping up with the all the records, must have
been a relieved Christian lady. On November 2, 1932, the church voted to
consolidate the church and the building fund accounts. Then, a vote was

4

taken for Mr. F. W. DeLong to be in charge of both.

Records remain of all conference minutes, but building fund records no longer exist. What we know is skimpy about specific events in the church's building history, money spent, and where purchases were made. A few records have been found in old WMU scrapbooks, newspaper clippings and memories from some of our life-long members. Windows were added to the church sanctuary and the Patterson Building as funds became available.

Following you will observe the location of the windows in our entire church including the Patterson Building and the Atrium. Some of the windows were placed in memory or in honor of members and/or community people. The windows were installed as they were completed.

FOYER WINDOWS

#1 H. D. WALLACE

   AND H. D. TANNER

Hugh D. Wallace married Miss Chester A. Davis on October 18,1883. In 1930, he is listed as living in the home of H. D. Tanner, along with Corinne Tanner, age 28. Mr. Wallace left our church on December 1, 1931.

Henry David Tanner was born February 26, 1875. He served in World War I. In 1930, he lived on West Washington Street. He was employed as an undertaker, and who was widowed at that time. He died September 29, 1941 and is buried at Alta Vista Cemetery.

#2	MRS. B. H. MOORE	Primary Dept. #5 – Elected – August 28, 1929.
	AND CLASS	Primary Dept. #6 - 8 Year old boys, 1930.
#3	HOUSE OF PRAYER	
#4	R. A.'S 1929	
#5	MR. & MRS.	Mr. Harris became a Deacon in April 1929,
	J. HOMER HARRIS	and served on the Finance Committee in 1930.
#6	W. H. STEWART	Building Committee – JUNE 7, 1925,
		Trustee - 1925
#7	CHARLES EDISON	
	BY A FRIEND	

The window bearing Charles Edison's name was give by a friend. He was on the building committee in 1925, and served as a trustee in 1926 and 1932. He served as Sunday School Secretary for many years. He also served as a Delegate to the Chattahoochee Baptist Association many times. From August 27, 1924, until his last entry on September 14, 1932, he served as Church Clerk.

In 1930, he was living on Chestnut Street with his wife, Adeline E. He worked as a pattern maker in an iron factory. He was born August 1, 1882, and died September 30, 1956. He is buried at Alta Vista Cemetery. He is remembered fondly for the following: IN CONFERENCE, JUNE 7, 1925,

"ON MOTION, THE CHURCH VOTED TO BUILD A NEW CHURCH. ALSO, THEY ACCEPTED THE PLANS AS SUBMITTED BY CHARLES EDISON."

#8   E. A. BURCHFIELD   Served as a Deacon – Elected April 26, 1926.

SANCTUARY WINDOWS

#9   WORSHIP

IN SPIRIT

#10   BAPTISMAL WINDOW   GIVEN BY THE WMU – 1930 – $275.

#11   GOD IS LOVE

#12 (a)   IN MEMORY OF   (b)

COL. WILLIAM MALONE JOHNSON   "HE KEPT THE FAITH"

1875-1918

This set of windows, on the organ and piano side, was purchased by

the Colonel William Malone Johnson family. Miss Alline Johnson was

his niece.

Colonel Johnson was a prominent lawyer, educator and church worker at the

First Baptist Church. The family purchased the window in 1929 in his honor. THE

GAINESVILLE NEWS published the news of his death on October 30, 1918.

#13 (a) MEN'S BIBLE CLASS   (b) J.E. OWEN,

1929   TEACHER

This set of windows, on the left side facing the sanctuary, was purchased

in honor of J.E. Owen, Teacher of the Men's Bible Class in 1929. He was

elected to this class on August 28, 1929. Mr. Owen was active in many of

Central's church activities. He served as Chorister from September 13, 1913,

7

to April 6, 1936. He served as a delegate to the Chattahoochee Baptist

Association, served on the church Finance Committee in 1927, 1928,

and 1931, and on the Building Fund 1932 and 1933. He was ordained as

a Deacon on March 30, 1930, and served as Church Treasurer.

#14 (a) MR. &. MRS. B.H. MOORE   (b) MARIE MOORE

This set of windows was purchased to honor Mr. and Mrs. B.H. Moore

and their daughter, Marie. Mr. Moore served as Church Treasurer from

October 1929 until 1932. He became a Deacon on October 7, 1925. He served

as a Trustee in 1926, 1930, and 1932. He also served as a delegate to the

Chattahoochee Baptist Association, on the Finance Committee 1929, 1930,

1932, and 1933, and as Church Treasurer from October 1929 until 1932.

Mrs. B.H. Moore taught Sunday School, Primary Department #5 teacher

elected August 28, 1929, and the Primary Department Class # 6 - 8 year old

boys in 1930. She also served on the Finance Committee.

#15 (a) MR. AND MRS.   (b) F.W. DELONG

This set honors Mr. and Mrs. F. W, DeLong. Mr. DeLong became a Deacon

in 1925. He served on the Finance Committee, as a delegate to the

Chattahoochee Baptist Association, elected as Church Treasurer in 1932

and 1933. He also served as a teacher in the Intermediate Sunday School

Class #12 in 1929, and Class #14 in 1930, and as a Trustee in 1932.

#16 (a) MR. AND MRS.   (b) T. O. CULPEPPER

Both Mr. and Mrs. T.O. Culpepper served as messengers to the Chattahoochee

Baptist Association, elected September 9, 1932. Mrs. Culpepper worked in the

Beginners Sunday School Department in 1929 in Class # 1, in 1930 Class # 3 and

was elected, on September 14, 1932, as Beginners Teacher and Superintendent.

#17 (a) E. A. BURCHFIELD   (b) AND FAMILY

Mr. Burchfield served our church in a number of capacities, from Chairman of

Deacons, first elected April 26, 1926, to a source of financial loans to our church

as early as 1920. He often served as a delegate to the Chattahoochee Baptist

Association, served on the Building Committee, the first Finance Committee, and

on the Pulpit Committee. Mrs. Burchfield taught the Women's Sunday School

Class, ages 24-35 in 1932. Marie Burchfield, daughter, taught the Beginners #2

1929, 1930 and 1932.

#18 (a) J. E. OWEN   (b) AND FAMILY

Mr. Owen was a faithful member. Window #13 (a) and (b) honored him as

as a teacher by the Men's Bible Class. This window honored his family and

their dedication to our young church.

#19 (a) FROM BEREANS,   (b) JUDGE WHEELER,

   FIRST BAPTIST CHURCH   TEACHER

   GAINESVILLE, GA. 29

Judge Wheeler was a beloved teacher of the Bereans Class at the First

9

First Baptist Church. The class is still in operation today. Shortly before

Mr. Martin Ellard's death, I spoke with him about Judge Wheeler. He told

me Judge Wheeler was a prominent lawyer for many years and worked

out of his law firm in the Jackson Building. The Jackson Building was constructed

in 1915 and was Gainesville and the area's first skyscraper.

#20 (a) EUZELIAN CLASS   #20 (b) WALKER AND MADGE MARTIN

1929   WILLA, HELEN, MARY & LINDA

Window (a) was purchased in 1929 by the ladies Euzelian Class taught

by Mr. R.L. Luther.

Window (b) was purchased by Helen Martin to honor our 125th anniversary.

Helen's father was killed in an accident in 1949. Her mother, Madge, died in June

2003. Mary, Helen's sister, died in 1999. Willa Martin and Linda Dover are still

serving God. Linda is an active participant at Central. Helen has been a member

of Central Baptist for more than fifty plus years.

Many of the Martin's have attended Central over its 130 year history

and can be found in the records located in the History Center above the

Pastor's office.

#21   ADULT I BIBLE CLASS

BOONE STRICKAND

TEACHER

Window #21 was dedicated to the Adult I Sunday School Class taught by

10

Boone Strickland. Boone attended Central when he was young, and later moved to work in other churches. They have one son, David and his wife Caroline, and two grandchildren Micah and Miranda.

In 2000, Boone and his wife, Ann Nix Strickland, returned to Central. Boone was an ordained Deacon at that time. They began a Sunday School Class literally from ground zero to a booming enrollment. Ann has worked in Vacation Bible School for many years. Boone was licensed to preach in 2004, and ordained to the Gospel Ministry on January 11, 2015. He became Associate Pastor in 2022.

#22   101 BIBLE CLASS

REV. WILBURN & WILLIE PEEPLES

Window #22 was dedicated to Rev. and Mrs. Willie Peeples by the 101 Sunday School Class. On July 11, 1965, Rev. Peeples was ordained by Central to the Gospel Ministry at the request of Zion Hill Baptist Church. For a number of years, he and his wife served other churches, and in their retirement years returned to Central. They became a blessing to all of us. His outstanding musical talent made him special to Central. He taught in the 101 Sunday School Class and was on the radio for a number of years. It was sad, but happy day when he went to be with the Lord on November 29, 2011. Mrs. Willie continued to be a faithful and much loved member of Central until her death on January 11, 2013. What a beautiful difference they made in the life of all who knew them. What a legacy they left for all of us!

#23   MRS. OLDEN MARTIN

#24   CRYAL O. MARTIN

#25   OLDEN MARTIN

Windows #23, 24, and 25 were dedicated to the Olden Martin family. The

parents were members of Central when it was located at the corner of

Maple and Myrtle Street. They lived with their son, Cryal O. Martin, on Grove

Street. Mrs. Olden (Della B.) Martin died August 31, 1988 and is buried in Alta

Vista Cemetery. Mr. Olden Martin was born December 21, 1891, and lived until

July, 1964. He is buried at Alta Vista Cemetery.

WINDOW ENTERING THE CHURCH SANCTUARY FROM THE ATRIUM

#26   Neal Alton Family

The Alton Family: Neal, father, Lois Ellis, mother, daughter, Jan, and Neal's

sister, Betty Alton, began attending Central in the 1950s. They were invited

by Grady Watson who was a member of the 101 Men's Bible Class. Mr. Neal,

Mr. Grady, and Ms. Betty, the pianist, formed a trio. They sang on the radio

each week, traveled to many gospel singings, and sang at New Horizons Nursing

home for many years. They became well known and Mr. Neal accompanied

them on the bass guitar. Mr. Neal was a member of 101 and continued singing

and playing the bass after Mr. Grady died and Ms. Betty moved away. Jan

was an active member of Central. She served on the stewardship committee and sang in the church choir.

Mr. Neal went into the Army before finishing high school. After World War II was over with his wife's help, he earned his GED from Lyman Hall High School. His wife, Lois Ellis Alton, was well qualified for the task. She graduated from Young Harris College and Emory University.

#27   FATHER AND MOTHER

BY HOWARD REED

Window #27 located outside the sanctuary small elevator room was given by Howard, the son of Mr. and Mrs. W. B. Reed to honor his parents. Mrs. Reed was elected and served as a financial worker.

PRAYER ROOM

#28   ROY, MARY & KAREN CROWE

The Crowe family, Roy, Mary and daughter Karen were active members at Central for a number of years. Karen taught Sunday School, and made beautiful things for the church and members. Mr. Roy led the Keenagers, (senior members) for many years. He also served as an usher.

#29   FLOYD FAMILY

LAWRENCE, DOT, JEFF, AND JUSTIN

A lifelong resident of Gainesville, Lawrence was born into the family of Will and Elizabeth Floyd. Six sisters were born into the Floyd family: Joyce, Becky, Wilma, Sandra, Brenda, and Gail. Lawrence attended Central Baptist Church as a child. He was also active in the youth programs. After high school, he married

Dot Mincey, a native Gainesville girl. They had one son, Jeff, and one grandson,

Justin.

Lawrence served in the Gainesville Fire Department for a number of years. He

was a dedicated fireman and retired in 1998 after 33years of service to the city.

In their senior years, Lawrence and Dot joined Central's fellowship and became

involved and served on numerous committees. Lawrence was ordained as a

Deacon in 2013 and continued to serve until his death on December 15, 2019.

WINDOW LEADING TO HIGH STREET

#30   MISS FINGER'S

CLASS NO. 13

Miss Lizzie Finger was the teacher of Class #13, and was elected August 28,

1929 to teach the Intermediate Class. Miss Finger was a faculty member at

Gainesville High School in 1931. She married Mr. Kennon J. Ward who was also

on the faculty at the school. He was born on August 5, 1907. They were

married on October 29, 1934. They had one child, William B. Ward.

She was active at Central as long as they lived in Gainesville. They moved to

Nashville, Tennessee where Mr. Ward served as a Captain in the U. S. Army. He

died on June 1, 1997, and is buried in the Nashville Cemetery, in Davidson County,

Tennessee. Lizzie was born September 19, 1907, and died December28, 1988.

Her parents were Hurbert Lee Finger and Retta Twitty Chamber Finger.

31   ALLINE JOHNSON

1877 – 1969

TREASURER OF BUILDING

AND

WINDOW FUND

1926 - 1932

Alline Johnson's name is spelled two different ways, one with one L and one with two. When a document she wrote was found, the mystery was solved. She signed her name Miss Alline Johnson. She was a very active member when our current church was being built. She wrote the first history of Hall County. At one time this document was housed at the Hall County Library. She was an active member of the Col. William Candler Chapter of the Daughters of the American Revolution. She was the chapter Regent from 1947-1949. Miss Alline served as the Treasurer of the Stained-glass Window Fund from 1925-1932. She died in 1969 and her funeral was conducted by Dr. Harold F. Green. She had no close of kin on her announcement.

FIRST FLOOR PATTERSON BUILDING - PASTOR'S OFFICE

#32   MRS. J.H. WALLACE

Mrs. J. H. Wallace, Florence M., her husband, John H., and daughter, Sylvia were members of Central in the 1920s. Sylvia was born May 5, 1897, and died January17, 1943. In 1920, they lived on Chestnut Street. They had a second daughter, Birtha, three sons, John. H., Linton. Mr. J. E. Wallace

died May 10, 1927.

#33   Mr. & MRS. J.C. BOWEN

   J. C. Bowen was born about 1874. He was first married when he was 19 years

old. His second marriage was on July 25, 1926, to Georgia Gravitte in Hall County.

According to the 1930 census they lived at 212 Davis Street. They had two

daughters Louise, age 18, and Cleo, age 15; and two sons W. C., age 12, and

James, age 9. Mr. Bowen was a cotton mill worker.

LIBRARY WINDOWS

#34   W.B. JOHNSON

   Mr. Johnson was elected to be a Deacon May 7, 1924.

#35   MRS. ANNIE E. JOHNSON

   Mrs. Johnson served as Sunday School Superintended for the Adult

Department in 1932.

#36   - BEGINNERS -

   MARIE BURCHFIELD

   Marie Burchfield taught the Beginners class #2 in 1929, 1930 and 1932.

#37   BEGINNERS - MRS. CULPEPPER

   Mrs. Culpepper worked with Beginners Sunday School Department, Class #1

in 1929, Class #3 in 1930, and was elected on September 14, 1932 as Beginners

Teacher and Superintendent.

CONFERENCE ROOM WINDOWS

#38   J. L. ALLISON

#39   MRS. J. L. ALLISON

Mr. and Mrs. J. L. Allison are honored in windows 37 and 38. John Lafayette,
(1874-1961) and Inez Kinsey Allison (1885-1970) were married in 1909 and had
seven children. The Allison's were actively involved in building the current
Central Baptist Church. J. L., a blacksmith and machinist, was one of
the men who dug out the basement of the church (without the aid of tractors,
backhoes, etc.). Inez and the ladies of the church did everything they could to
help pay for pews, church furniture, supplies, etc. Often the ladies collected
all items they did not need and held rummage sales to raise money. Inez was a
member of the choir, WMU and taught 9 year old Sunday School boys for almost
40 years. A number of men who attended Central Baptist as former youth boys
have stated that Mrs. Allison led them to Christ when they were in her Sunday
School class. She had "her boys" memorize John 3:16, which they recited every
Sunday. Inez was known to be "at the church every time the doors were open"
until she became physically and mentally unable to attend. Several of the Allison
children followed in their parents' footsteps as they grew up, married and
brought up their children at Central Baptist Church.

Children of J. L. and Inez Allison: William P. (Bill) Allison, Cora Lee Allison
Quinn, Ruby Allison Maddox, William (Buck) Allison, Grace Allison Allen,

Louise Allison Stargel, and Clara Allison Dolson. There were 16 grandchildren.

Margie Allison Webb was one of the grandchildren and daughter of Buck Allison.

Thank you, Margie, for this lovely tribute to your family and for still being here at

Central! We must not forget Becky Quinn Herrington whose mother was

Cora Lee Allison Quinn. Becky is still here, too!

#40   THOMAS G. & MILDRED B.

DAVIS & FAMILY

Mildred and Tommy were long-time members of Central Baptist Church. They

raised three children at the church, Steve, Scott and Susan. Tommy was

active until his death in 2003. Mildred taught 3rd, 4th, and 5th graders in Sunday

School until her brief illness and death in 2016. She served on the Lord's Supper

and the Baptismal Committees.

#41   JACK & COLEEN PETHEL

BY THE CHILDREN

Jack and Coleen Pethel came to Central in 1949. They were giving and very

active members. They raised three children at Central; Stan, Nancy and

Margie. Jack served as a Deacon, Choir member, Sunday School Director and

Teacher, Building Committee Chairman, and 101 Sunday School Pianist. Coleen

worked with Girls in Action, and worked as a Sunday School Teacher and has

been Sunday School Secretary and Teacher for sixty plus years. She is still serving

as the Sunday School Secretary. Jack went to be with Lord in 2016.

#42   IN MEMORY OF

DONALD JAMES STRICKLAND

BY JIM & DIANA LATIMER

Donald James Strickland was born on February 14, 1943. He married Ann Martin. Their children are Scott, Wendi, April and Sterling. He was a dedicated member of Central's Choir. He was faithful in rehearsal and loved music. He went to be with the Lord on February 1, 2009.

He was employed by Jim and Diane Latimer owners of Industrial Pipe Line of Gainesville. They dedicated the window in his memory.

#43   HARVEY & BETTY ROOKS

FAMILY

Harvey and Betty Rooks came to Central in September, 1960. They raised three children in Central, twins, Keith and Faith, and Adina. Betty has taught teen girls and senior adults. She served as Church Secretary and WMU Director for several years. Harvey taught junior and adult couples Sunday School Classes. Harvey serves as a Deacon, Trustee, and on the Building and Grounds Committee.

RESTROOM BEYOND THE CONFERENCE ROOM

------One window unmarked.

This is a bathroom location and was once a Minister of Youth space.

19

SUNDAY SCHOOL DIRECTOR'S OFFICE

------Two windows unmarked.

SECOND FLOOR PATTERSON BUILDING

HISTORY ROOM

RESOURCE ROOM---Two windows have been removed. (Now in the Atrium)

TIME LINE ROOM---Two windows removed. (Now in the Atrium)

--One window unmarked.

#44   W.B. REED'S CLASS

W. B. Reed's Class window #44, is located on the second floor in the Patterson

Building. Mr. Reed taught Sunday School Class #15 in 1929, Class #12 in 1930,

served on the Financial Committee, as a Trustee 1926 – 1932, delegate

to the Chattahoochee Baptist Association and was an ordained Deacon.

WINDOW AT THE BACK OF THE LARGE ROOM IN THE HISTORY ROOM

#45   ROWLAND Q. LEAVEL – MOVED FROM OUTSIDE THE CHURCH

SANCTUARY ENTRY – WINDOW - NOW IN THE HISTORY CENTER.

Dr. Rowland Q. Leavel was a pastor at the First Baptist Church. He preached

the sermon for the Deacon Ordination Service, Sunday, June 20, 1929, when

J.W.A. Mooney was ordained into the ministry. R.A. Hawkins, J.H. Smith,

J. Homer Harris and Rufus McMahan were also ordained as Deacons.

Dr. Leavel also participated, March 30, 1930, when J.C. Owen, D.L. Payne,

Ray Simpson, and Horace T. Lenderman were ordained.

VINTAGE CLOTHING ROOM----2 unmarked windows.

BOILER ROOM

#46   IN MEMORY OF

J. RUSSELL STOVALL

James Russell Stovall was born March 26, 1910, in Forsyth County, Georgia.

He died on March 10, 1927, at the age of sixteen. He was buried at Alta Vista

Cemetery where his parents were later laid to rest. His parents were Charles A., and

Mamie Lee Stovall. They lived on Broad Street according to the 1920 Census.

MUSIC REHEARSAL FACILITY

------Small rooms 1,2,5,7 are unmarked.

#47   (Small room #3)   IN MEMORY OF

VALERIA BURCHFIELD

(Ida) Valarie Burchfield was the daughter of E. A. (Elie Andrew) and Mary E.

Herron Burchfield. Valarie was eight years old in the 1900 Census. She died on

January 23 in 1908, at the age of sixteen. The window was given in her honor.

#48   (Small room #4)   IN MEMORY OF

B. F. ROBERTS

B. F. Roberts was quite active in church affairs. He served as a Church Delegate

for some activities, and accepted appointments to deal with church business.

Most notably, he served as the Church Treasurer for many years until health issues prevented him from serving in this capacity. In appreciation for his service, Mr. Roberts was paid $10.00 per quarter until his death.

#49   (Small room #5)   IN MEMORY OF

W. D. PIERCE

W.D. (Willie) Pierce married Alice Shadburn on June 1, 1894. Alice was born June 6, 1874. In 1920, they lived on W. College Avenue. They had six children. One daughter, Monttee, was seventeen years old at the time. Monttee was born September 8, 1902, and died October 18, 1928. She was a domestic worker and lived at 411 Grove Street. She was buried at Alta Vista Cemetery. By 1939, the family had moved to Atlanta, Georgia. Alice Shadburn, mother, died while she was living in Knoxville, Tennessee in 1947 as reported by her daughter, Dartruce Pierce.

#50 (Small room #6)   IN MEMORY OF

J. W. JACKSON

J. W. Jackson was born in Habersham, Georgia on January 8, 1919. He was employed at a Gainesville Cotton Mill. He was 21 when he was honorably discharged from the military.

SECOND FLOOR PATTERSON BUILDING ON THE ELEVATOR SIDE

#51   (Elevator entry)   MEN'S BIBLE CLASS

FIRST BAPTIST CHURCH   (No information found)

-----ladies dressing room-----One unmarked window

22

#52   W. K. (Warren) Owens And L. A. (Alizabeth) Coker Owens

A window on the Main Street side has been purchased by Miss Loraine Davis to honor her grandparents who had the first wedding at Central. Her grandparents were W. K. (Warren Knox) Owens and L. A. (Alizabeth) Coker Owens.

Dr. Harold Fredrick Green wrote in his book, NOT MADE FOR DEFEAT...The History of the Central Baptist Church 1890 ---1974 on page 30 the following:

> "A significant "first" took place 0n October 22, 1891 in the church
> family when "Sister" L. A. Coker united in holy wedlock, at her
> father's home, to W. K. Owens with pastor Barrett officiating. This
> was the first wedding in the Church and the first for Barrett as pastor."

Warren and Alizabeth had five children. They named them William Knox (often called Ray), Fred, Irene, Ross, and Warren Herbert. W. K. built a log Cabin off the Athens Highway near Oak Grove Baptist Church for his family. Sadly Warren Knox died of typhoid fever when his oldest child, Ray, was 8 years old. Warren Knox is buried in the Oak Grove Baptist Church Cemetery. His grave is marked by a large stone that Ray found and lovingly placed on his grave.

The family seemed to have prospered. They all married, had children, and continued to look after their mother, Alizabeth, who never remarried. Alizabeth lived to be one month and one day short of 77 years. She died on March 12, 1951, and is buried at Alta Vista Cemetery in Gainesville, Georgia.

23

#53   DEACONS   2013 - 2014

New deacons: Clarence A. Barnett, Dee Bell, Lawrence Floyd – Ordained September 8, 1913.

Other deacons listed: Ray Martin, Sam Curtis, Harvey Rooks, Boone Strickland, Walter Smith, Hy Reynolds, Y. J. Seay, Jim DeLay, John Lackey, George Reese, Tony Walker, and George Wiley.

#54   IN HONOR AND MEMORY

CENTRAL DEACONS

This window pays tribute to all deacons who have served Central over the last 130 years and beyond.

#55   JACK & LOIS HURT FAMILY

Central was the first church Jack Hurt attended in the 1940s. He is a member of Gideons International. He served as the Brotherhood Director for several years, and his wife Lois is involved in Women on Missions. Jack and Lois moved their letter to Central a few years ago.

#56 & 57

DON AND ANITA MARTIN

Both Don and Anita were born and raised in Gainesville. Don's mother, Lillie Woodall Martin and family were active members of Central from 1948 to 1957.

(1) Don's sister, Eleanor Martin Fortner, was born January 14, 1933, and died March 24, 2021. She was living at the Oaks at the time of her death.

(2) Elizabeth Martin London, sister, was born October23, 1938. She lives in Cornelia, Georgia.

(3) Don's brother, Riley Leon Martin, was born June 1, 1927, and died March 9, 1992. He was a Gainesville City Policeman from June 1, 1952, until Oct. 29, 1972.

----Don's father was Riley A. Martin born July 28, 2003, and died Jan. 27, 1946.

---- Walter J. Head and Henrietta Woodall Head and daughter, Mary Lou

Head, were all members. They were Don's uncle and aunt. Everyone lived on the corner of Summit and Grove Street with goats, chickens and milk cows.

--- Anita's mother was Doris Haynes Cain. She passed away at age forty-one from a brain tumor. Anita was an only child. Her grandparents were R.M. and Cora Lou Haynes. Her father was Wayne Cain. She was a member at Trinity Methodist Church, built by her grandfather, for many years. She was also a member at Emmanuel and Central Baptist. Don and Anita have two daughters, Julie and Ann. They moved from Gainesville to the Atlanta area in 1962.

#58   REV. BOB THOMPSON &

         BETTY SUE THOMPSON

Rev. Bob Thompson served as Central's Interim Music Director in 1956 and 1958 when Dr. Scott Patterson was interim Pastor. Betty Sue Smith, his future wife, was saved and baptized at Central. They both attended Truett McConnell College. He married Betty Sue, and served as a faculty member at Lyman

Hall School where he taught Jan Cobb's husband.

He and Betty Sue have visited Central from time to time. He served as pastor at some local churches and in other areas. They taught English in Korea, also at the Yanti University in China. Today they live in the Tifton, Georgia area. They have grown older, but still share their strong faith.

#59   CONTRIBUTED BY

CENTRAL'S CHOIR

At the time of this marking, Mr. Eddie Simmons was Central's Music Minister. He passed away on December 28, 2020.

---Four windows are unmarked. The four windows on the Main Street side of the Atrium were the ones removed from the outside of the church where the History Center is located.

THIRD LANDING – ATRIUM

#60   ERNEST

REYNOLDS

FAMILY

This window was marked to honor the Ernest Reynolds Family by his son, Hyman (Hy) Reynolds. There were three children, first, Robert Budgy, his wife, and three children Charlie, Robert, and Catherine. The second child, Hy and his wife Teresa (T.C.) and two sons: Drew and Chad. The third child, Kelly and husband, Al Marasso, had three children Nicole, Ali and Julie.

The Hy Reynolds family still attends Central. They are active in various

church activities, and contribute to the life and growth of the Church.

Mr. Ernest and wife Frances West were married at Central Baptist Church on

May 24, 1957.

The happy couple in the photograph above is Mr. Ernest Reynolds and wife
Frances West Reynolds whose wedding was at Central on May 24, 1957. They are the
parents of Hy Reynolds.

This historian can report that Central Baptist Church is one of the most beautiful
and pleasing churches for a wedding. As a wedding director, it was a moving time
to watch as the ceremony came together successfully. The largest wedding in my
memory was Shanda Tyner and Eddie Millwood 's beautiful wedding. The church
sanctuary and the balcony were full of excited and happy people.

FOYER   SANCTUARY WINDOWS

#6   W. H. STEWART

#8   E. A. BURCHFIELD

#12 (a)   IN MEMORY OF

COL. WILLIAM MALONE JOHNSON

1875-1918

#13 (a) MEN'S BIBLE CLASS
(b) J.E. OWEN,
              1929
    TEACHER

#14 (a) MR. & MRS. B.H. MOORE
        (b) MARIE MOORE

#15 (a) MR. AND MRS.
            (b) F.W. DELONG

#16 (a) MR. AND MRS.

    (b) T. O. CULPEPPER

#17 (a) E. A. BURCHFIELD
        (b) AND FAMILY

28

See pages 9 and 10 in BOOK II

#18 (a) J. E. OWEN

(b) AND FAMILY

#19 (a) FROM BEREANS,

FIRST BAPTIST CHURCH

GAINESVILLE, GA. 29

(b) JUDGE WHEELER,

TEACHER

PICTURES GLEANED FROM OLD NEWSPAPER CLIPPINGS, OLD SCRAPBOOKS, ETC. ARE NOT ALWAYS EASY TO FIND OR REPRODUCE. IT IS BETTER TO HAVE AN IMAGE THAN "NOT PICTURED."

#20 (b) WALKER

LINDA
MARY
WILLA
HELEN
MADGE MARTIN

BALCONY WINDOWS

Boone & Ann Strickland

#21 ADULT I BIBLE CLASS

BOONE STRICKAND

TEACHER

WINDOW ENTERING THE CHURCH SANCTUARY FROM THE ATRIUM

#26 Neal Alton Family

Wilburn & Willie Peeples

#22 101 BIBLE CLASS
REV. WILBURN & WILLIE PEEPLES

#23 MRS. OLDEN MARTIN

#24 CRYAL O. MARTIN

#25 OLDEN MARTIN

29

CATHERINE – NEAL ALTON – JAN COBB

PRAYER ROOM

#28   ROY, MARY & KAREN CROWE

#29   FLOYD FAMILY

LAWRENCE, DOT, JEFF, AND Justin

MISS FINGER

#30   MISS FINGER'S

CLASS NO. 13

#31   ALINE JOHNSON

1877 – 1969

TREASURER OF BUILDING

WINDOW FUND

CONFERENCE ROOM WINDOWS

#38   J. L. ALLISON

#39   MRS. J. L. ALLISON

#40   THOMAS G. & MILDRED B.

Thomas & Mildred Davis,
Susan, Steven & Scott

DAVIS & FAMILY

30

#41   JACK & COLEEN PETHEL

BY THE CHILDREN

Don & Ann Strickland

#42   IN MEMORY OF

DONALD JAMES STRICKLAND   #43   HARVEY & BETTY ROOKS

BY JIM & DIANA LATIMER   FAMILY

#45   ROWLAND Q. LEAVEL

A window on the Main Street side has been purchased by Miss Loraine Davis to

honor her grandparents who had the first wedding at Central.

#52   W. K. (Warren) Owens And L. A. (Alizabeth) Coker Owens

Loraine Davis

ATRIUM

#55   JACK & LOIS HURT FAMILY

#56 & 57

DON AND ANITA MARTIN

#58

REV. BOB THOMPSON &

BETTY SUE THOMPSON

31

#59   CONTRIBUTED BY

      CENTRAL'S CHOIR

At the time of this marking, Mr. Eddie Simmons was Central's Music

Minister. He passed away on December 28, 2020.

THIRD LANDING – ATRIUM

#60   ERNEST

         REYNOLDS

         FAMILY

Teresa and Hy Reynolds

Frances Reynolds

NOTES OF APPRECIATION AND COPYRIGHT STATEMENT

Many Thanks

REBECCA MORGAN

LARRY DYER

LAVERNE SUTTON

Without the three of you, there would be no TO DREAM AGAIN book. Thanks and much appreciation for your help in getting this project completed.

Bud Savage is a very good and self-taught artist. He has

sketched and drawn hundreds of houses, churches and

other buildings in North Georgia and beyond. Bud has

captured the people of Central Baptist Church in both

fun and serious poses. Bud serves as the photographer

at Central Baptist Church.

Bud Savage—Photographer extraordinaire!

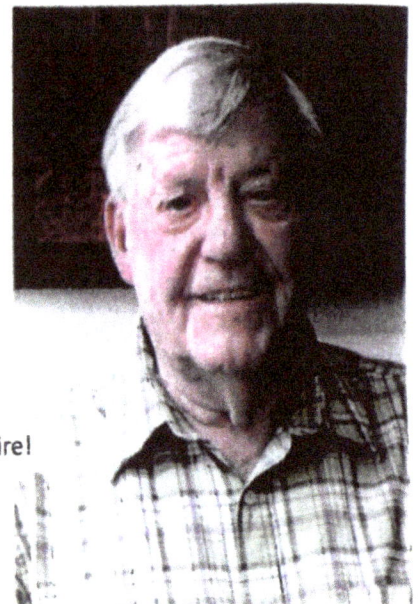

About 95% of the information in the writing of this book came from Central's own Conference Minute Books, deeds, records, and other church documents. There were interviews and conversations with members who had been at the church for many years. Information was sought from a newspaper editor and other newspaper and knowledgeable individuals about copyright obligations.

CONCLUDING STATEMENT

WE AS A CARING, DEDICATED PEOPLE MUST WORK TOWARD THE TASK OF REACHING
AN INNER CITY AND COMMUNITY FOR CHRIST. WE MUST BECOME COMMITTED TO DREAM
AGAIN---TO COME ALIVE! DREAMS HAVE AN IMPACT WHEN SET IN MOTION. WE MUST
LEAD PEOPLE INTO BECOMING A DYNAMIC FORCE FOR THE KINGDOM'S WORK. WE MUST
LOOK TO GOD THROUGH THE LEADERSHIP OF PASTOR MIKE TAYLOR TO MAKE THIS A REALITY.

It has been a labor of love searching for any bits and pieces of those who
were blessed with the dedication of a beautiful stained glass WINDOW IN THEIR
memory or honor. Have you ever looked at the beautiful windows and wondered
who some of the names of people from the past really were? This publication
will answer some of your questions.   Love and blessings, Helen.

EPILOGUE

After reading the preceding history of Central Baptist Church, you may be wondering what the future holds for this Lighthouse, this Soul-Saving Station that has been in existence since 1890. Allow me to refer you to God's Word for the answer to that question: "For I know the plans I have for you declares the LORD, plans to prosper you and not to harm you, plans to give you hope and a future."

(Jeremiah 29: 11)

We rejoice in knowing that God has a plan to preserve and protect this church that He loves, this church for which He died. You may rest assured that His perfect plàn includes a time of great blessing. Friends, God did not call us to be successful, but He has called us to be faithful. When we are faithful, He has promised to pour out blessings beyond measure.

In closing, may I remind you that there is nothing God can not do. Our future is as certain and as sure as the very promises we find in His Holy Word. My prayer is that you will hide this word in your heart and never forget it: "I can do all things through Christ who strengthens me."   (Philippians 4: 13)

God Bless,

Brother Don Elrod

INTERIM MUSIC MINISTER
Don Elrod

9 798823 018050